· D

Ri

Th

your amazi over

Controlled Chaos
A Memoir

Love,
Jenny

Jenny Guiton

I have changed some of the names of people and places for their anonymity.

Copyright © 2012 by Jenny Guiton

Createspace.com

Nonfiction Memoir

www.controlledchaos-jenny.blogspot.com

Controlled Chaos, A Story of Redemption

ISBN-13: 978-1468136722

ISBN-10: 1468136720

Front cover photography and graphics by Jenna Guiton

This book would not have been possible without the encouragement, support, and hard work of many people.

Thank you to my kids for giving me the motivation to do the hard work it took to become a better mom. Dad and I are so proud of you.

Thank you to my husband who has always believed in me and stuck with me for better or for worse for more than twenty-one years. I don't know what I would do without you.

Thank you to Jen, my therapist for being kind, compassionate, and patient during my therapy and for helping me with the details of this book.

Thank you to Ann for all the help you've given me to make this book possible, and for always being there for me. I can't put into words how much you mean to me.

Thank you to Nancy for your mentorship and your friendship and all the other roles you fill in my life. No one has directed me toward God and His word like you have. I couldn't have made this journey without your direction, encouragement, prayers and the way you celebrate every one of my little achievements.

Thank you to the two book clubs that read my book in the early phases and gave me vital feedback.

Thank you to all my friends who've supported me. It wasn't easy to write with so much emotion, but all of your positive feedback helped me continue writing when I wanted to quit.

Thank you to my brothers and sisters for being the most amazing siblings in the world. I love that we know we'd do anything and everything for each other, and we do.

Thank you to my mom and dad. Life growing up was chaotic, but I know you did the best you could.

And thank you to God for giving me an opportunity and the strength to change.

For my amazing kids,
Andy, Jenna, and Johnny
I love you

Session 1

I'm standing, facing a wall with my back toward Jen. Jen's my therapist. It's my first time here. I'm nervous because she's watching me and waiting. I'm staring at four long shelves that stretch the length of the room. Two shelves are filled with little toy people: action figures, Playskool people, Disney characters, etc. The other shelves have props like trees, rocks, fences, and animals. There are hundreds of items on the wall and more in the containers on the floor. I'm supposed to pick out some things that represent how I feel. I don't know how I feel. I don't want to know how I feel. The room feels like it is a hundred degrees. I want to run out the door or hide under the table.

I slip one of my shaky hands into my pocket. I look at the shelves. There are so many toys. I have to do something, but I can't move. I can't breathe. I can't think. I turn to look at Jen. I cringe a little waiting for her impatience to flair, but she is calm. Her hand is resting under her chin. Her eyes are big and brown. She looks at me and smiles. I swallow and exhale. I didn't realize I was holding my breath. It seems she could wait all day for me to make a decision. Maybe I can do this.

I step toward the wall hoping it forces something to jump out at me. My eyes move along the shelf past each of the characters until I spot a little Pocahontas figure. I pick her up. I feel a little better having made a decision. I look over the other figures. I pick out two boy figures and a girl for my kids. I skim the shelves and grab a miniature champagne bottle, some trees, a fence, and a miniature gun. I walk back to the table and place the items into the sandbox which sits on the table between us. After placing everything in the sandbox I slide onto a hard plastic chair. Jen looks in the sandbox and starts asking me questions.

"Who is Pocahontas?"

"That's me."

"Why did you choose Pocahontas?"

"Because she belongs outside, in the woods… not locked up."

"Do you feel locked up?"

"Yes."

"Why?"

"I'm married, and I have kids."

I stare at my shoes which are tapping on the floor beneath me.

"So, you have responsibilities."

"I don't want any more responsibilities."

I stare at the tray because I don't know what else to do. I don't want to be here, but I don't have anywhere else to go. I want a different life, but I'm scared to death of what it will take to get one.

"Why don't you tell me more about Pocahontas?"

I run my hands down my jeans. I can hear my heartbeat in my ears. I feel like a wild animal trapped in a corner. I'm trying to resist the urge to fight my way out. Jen is not the enemy. I look above her at the wall and force myself to say something.

"When I was growing up we lived by the woods. I went there a lot to get away."

"What were you getting away from?"

There is a long pause.

"My house."

Dozens of pictures and emotions flash through my head. They are scattered and disjointed, and I can't seem to filter through any of it. I desperately want Jen to see what's in my head, but I don't know how to let her inside. I have to think of something else. There is a long pause. I keep thinking Jen is going to fill the space, but she doesn't seem troubled by the silence. I'm dying to tell her that I want to be held. I'd give up eating for a week if I could curl up in a ball and rest my head on her lap. I want to be five again so it's okay to cry.

"I was the oldest of seven kids. Our house was pretty chaotic."

I'm staring at the sand in the tray. She remains silent. I take a deep breath.

3

"My dad worked a lot. If he came home late it meant he had gone to the bar."

I want to tell her how scary it was when he came home drunk, but my mind goes blank. I try to shake some mental cobwebs loose.

"My mom was gone a lot, too. She didn't have a job, but she volunteered at church."

I take my eyes off the sand tray and look at Jen. She has been looking at me the whole time. I'm not used to someone focusing on me for that long. She moves on to the next thing in the tray.

"What is the bottle?"

"It's a wine bottle."

"Is that what you drank?"

"That was my first choice, but anything would do."

"When did you start drinking?"

"My dad gave me my first beer when I was ten."

"Ten?"

"Yeah, but I didn't start drinking regularly until I was fourteen."

Jen looks at the tray again and points to the little people.

"Are these your children?"

"Yes."

"Tell me about them."

My chest tightens. I close my eyes. My feet start tapping. I push away the pain and focus on the facts.

"Andy is nine. He's in third grade. Jenna is seven. She's in second grade, and Johnny is five. He's in kindergarten. I was homeschooling them until I went to treatment, so school is still pretty new to them."

"Why did you place them in the corner of the sand tray?"

"Because I feel far away from them."

"Why do you feel so far away?"

"It's like there's always this barrier between us. I can physically touch them and hold them, but I never feel close to them."

Jen pauses. She seems so content in the silence. My heart is beating out of my chest. I need her to say something. She looks at the tray again.

"What's your husband's name?"

"JB."

"Is there a reason you didn't put JB in the tray?"

My eyes immediately look over all the pieces in the tray. I didn't even notice I left him out. I wonder what that

5

means. I wonder what she thinks it means. I go with the easy answer.

"He's not home very much. He works a lot."

"Why don't you go choose a figure off the wall for him?"

I stand up and turn around to face the wall again. I look over all the figures, but nothing stands out. I hate the feeling that she's watching me and waiting. I take a step closer. My eyes scan each shelf. I want to pick one, but nothing fits.

"There's nothing here that works for him."

"Just choose the closest thing."

I look over the figures again. The super heroes are out. The little Playskool people are definitely out. None of the other male figures are even close. Then I see a row of villains. There's an action figure that is three times the size of all the others. He is dark blue and black and has a web of ice all around him. I grab him off the shelf and put him in the tray. The villain towers over Pocahontas.

"This is JB?"

"Sort of."

"Is he a lot bigger than you?"

"His personality is."

"What do you mean?"

"He's intimidating. I can't really say what I'm thinking to him."

"Why not?"

"When I try, I always end up being shut down, like my brain won't work anymore. I don't know how to explain it."

"So, nothing gets resolved?"

"Right."

"Do you feel safe at home?"

It takes me a second to understand what she's asking.

"Yes. It's not like that. He's a good guy. I'm not physically intimidated by him. I just freeze up when we argue."

Jen nods her head, looks down at the tray and back up at me again.

"What is the fence?"

"It's supposed to be a brick wall, but I couldn't find a wall."

"Okay, what is the brick wall?"

"It's the wall between me and other people."

"Any people in particular?"

"No. Everyone is on the other side of the wall."

"So, you feel lonely."

My chest tightens again. It feels like someone is squeezing my heart like a balloon popping contest. I take a deep breath. My foot starts tapping in place.

"Yeah, I do."

I notice my whole leg is now tapping and I force myself to stop.

"How about the gun?"

My foot starts tapping again.

"That's a way to escape if I need it."

"Have you ever tried to escape that way?"

My foot taps faster.

"No, but there were times I wanted to."

"Kill yourself?"

There's silence. It feels like the air has been sucked out of the room. Sometimes the thought of killing myself is the only thing that relieves the torture in my mind. I picture myself driving into oncoming traffic or through the cross bars onto the railroad tracks. I can see myself hanging in the garage, but I don't want a slow, painful death. I already have that. I want a quick, painless ending. I settle on a large pile of lethal pills. It seems like the easiest way. I swallow the pile, then lie down on a bed of leaves and look up at the sky and wait. The image temporarily relieves the torture in my mind.

"Yeah."

"Do you want to kill yourself now?"

This question is different than all the others. I don't feel she wants to know more about me at this point. I feel she needs to know whether or not I am suicidal. If I answer this wrong I could wind up in the psych ward. I would lie about it if I was because I'm not willing to get locked up again like in the treatment center, but I don't need to.

"No. The antidepressants are working now that I stopped drinking."

The air seeps back into the room. We're at the end of my first session. I walk out the door, down the long hallway and get into my van. I like Jen. She listens to me. But, I am paying her to listen. I'm not sure what to think. I'm tired of thinking.

I start the engine of my car and the radio is playing *Little Red Corvette*. There's a Harley Davidson dealership across the street, and the billboard is screaming at me to come trade in my minivan for a motorcycle and ride away from everyone and everything. I take a deep breath as I contemplate the idea of running away. I drop my head on the steering wheel. My shoulders feel like bags of sand. I look at the clock. I have to get home. My kids will be home from school soon. I need to be there for them.

Session 2

I pull into the parking lot. I'm ten minutes early. I've been anxious about seeing Jen for a couple of days now. I think she's my bridge out of isolation, but I hate talking about myself. My heart races faster as I walk down the hall toward the office. I meet people in the hallway and wonder if they know I'm heading to see my therapist. I feel like I'm wearing a sign with huge words printed on it: DEPRESSED ALCOHOLIC. I smile faintly at people, look at the floor, and walk to the end of the hall.

I wonder if I should really be here. I look around and blink my eyes wondering if it's just a bad dream, but nothing happens and my reality is sharp, raw, and abrasive. As I wonder if I'm in the right place, I think of my week in the treatment center.

The Chemical Dependency wing is on the second floor of an old Catholic hospital. A smoky film covers the walls and the grey carpet looks like it may have been a shade of blue at one time. Down the hall is the lounge where we eat, watch TV, and do most of our group therapy. There is a huge variety of people in treatment with me. Jane is in a wheelchair hooked to an oxygen tank with tubes up her nose. She is here to quit drinking so she can see her granddaughter again. Jeff is a lawyer. He's short with graying hair and glasses. He is here to save his law practice and his family. Ronald looks like he's homeless, but when he plays the piano in the lounge on our breaks I wonder what his life used to look like. Troy is a drug dealer who's trying to decide if he is willing to give up his nice lifestyle for a minimum wage job. I am a suburban housewife who goes to church and homeschools my kids. Well, I was homeschooling them. I'm not anymore, but I don't fit in with these people. I know I don't belong here. We're sitting in a circle, and it's Matt's turn to tell his story.

Matt is an annoying, obnoxious teenager. He interrupts every conversation, every instructor and talks through every video. None of us like him. Jeff and Ronald got in a yelling match with Matt yesterday because he wouldn't stop talking while we were watching a video. Today is our first group sharing time together. We go around the circle talking about how we got here. Matt starts talking. He was young when he started doing drugs. His parents were divorced. When he couldn't quit using, his mom kicked him out of the house. He went to live with his aunt, but soon she was threatening to kick him out, too. One day his aunt found him on the shower floor passed out and bleeding. He had been using a hallucinogen and thought worms were crawling out of his arms. He panicked and used a razor blade to cut the worms off. She brought him to the hospital and that's how he ended up here.

As he finishes his story the mood in the room changes. He has answered all the questions we haven't asked. I want to give him a hug and tell him it will be okay. Later we're watching a video that explains only 20 percent of people who go through treatment stay sober for any length of time. I think of this kid and wonder if there is any hope for him. How could life turn out like this for someone? Would I have turned out any different had I grown up in

11

his place? I don't think so, and my heart aches for him because I know what it feels like to be alone and misunderstood. We all go around and share our stories. As we finish, I don't wonder if I belong here anymore. It's the first time in my life that I feel like I completely belong. These people understand me like no one ever has.

I'm back in the hallway of the office building looking at the counseling sign on the door. I take a deep breath as I realize that yes, I am in the right place.

The outer door of Jen's office opens into a waiting area. A bell rings as I open the door. There are three offices including Jen's and the play therapy room where we were last week. Jen's door is open and I hear her voice.

"Come on in."

I walk by the play room and into her office. Jen is sitting in an arm chair. She has a small build, and as she crosses her legs, she hardly takes up any space on her little chair. Her hair is brown and curly, and she has a warm smile.
The only other place to sit is the swivel chair at her desk or the couch. I assume I'm supposed to sit on the couch. I sit down and sink into the cushions. I feel like I'm stuck. I move around trying to sit up further, but I can't. I give up and try to sit still. I feel like I'm drowning.

I look around the office. There are plaques on the wall stating Jen's qualifications as a therapist. Two windows open to the parking lot. The shades are mostly closed. A whiteboard is on the wall to my left. A small bookshelf holds various titles from co-dependence to grief to marriage and family. Two end tables flank the couch.

They both hold a lamp and on one there's a box of Kleenex.

"How are you feeling today?"

How am I feeling? I stare at the wall behind her. My thoughts are like distorted images in a thick fog. She opens a folder and hands me a piece of paper with rows of funny cartoon faces. There's a descriptive feeling word beneath each face. The page is titled "Feelings Chart." I look at each of the faces on the chart until I see one I might feel.

"Anxious."

"What are you anxious about?"

Everything makes me anxious, but I try to think of something I can say.

"Being here in your office."

"Anything else besides being in my office?"

I think for a minute. My heart is racing.

"I am going on my son's field trip this week."

"What about the trip makes you anxious?"

"I haven't been out much since I went to treatment."

"Maybe this will be good for you."

I don't say anything, but I don't care if it will be good for me or not. I'm scared to have a normal conversation with anyone. I don't even remember the last time I had a normal conversation. Depression and addiction have swallowed my life, and I feel like I'm in a foreign country trying to speak a foreign language. I don't know how to talk to my closest friends, let alone another mom from Andy's school.

I wonder what other moms would think if they knew I was an alcoholic. Can they tell from my eyes that I'm depressed and anxious and have a hard time getting out of bed in the morning? What if they ask me why my son is coming into third grade halfway through the year? I can't just say I was homeschooling him and then had to enroll him at the last minute before I was put in treatment. I don't know how to articulate this to Jen, so I stare at the floor between us.

"Let's have you do a personality test."

She goes to her file cabinet and pulls out a sheet of questions.

"This is the short version of the Myers-Briggs Personality test. Just answer the questions to the best of your ability."

She hands me the paper and a pen. I've filled out so much paperwork and answered so many questions in treatment that I don't think twice. I take the pen and read the first question.

A) I communicate with enthusiasm, B) I keep my enthusiasm to myself, or C) I'm really in between.

I wonder if I'm supposed to answer the questions as I feel now or how I felt before my life imploded, when I was still positive and happy. I used to communicate with enthusiasm. I used to be the life of the party. I can't remember what enthusiasm feels like. Maybe I should write that I'm in between. But what does "in between" mean? I wonder if they put that there to see whether or not I can make a decision. I don't want to appear indecisive. I look ahead to the next question;

A) I set and respect fixed goals and work toward achieving them on time, B) My goals are open-ended and subject to change as new information becomes available, or C) I'm really in-between.

What if I don't have any goals? This is going to be harder than I thought. I mentally throw my hands in the air and start choosing whichever answer strikes me first.

Jen is writing something down and I wonder how long this will take me. I wonder whether she's wondering how long this will take me and if it makes a difference how long it takes. Maybe the length of time it takes factors into my personality. Now I've wasted time thinking about it, and it will take more time! I need to focus on the questions and stop wondering what she's thinking. That's her job. She's probably not thinking about me at all. She's probably making out a grocery list.

I check the last box and give her the paper. She does a quick tally.

"You're an ENFP, which stands for extrovert, intuitive, feeling and perceiving. An extrovert is someone who gets energy by being with other people. Intuitive means you

15

are more inclined to make decisions with your gut than with sound evidence. Feeling means you make decisions mostly by what you feel rather than what you think, and perceivers go with the flow versus someone who likes to have a plan of attack."

I wonder how I can be classified as feeling if I have to look at a chart to figure it out. She continues to read a little information about the ENFP personality type.

"ENFP's are both idea-people and people-people, who see everyone and everything as part of an often bizarre cosmic whole. They have a great deal of zany charm, which can ingratiate them to the more stodgy types in spite of their unconventionality. They are outgoing, fun, and genuinely like people. As mates, they are warm, affectionate and disconcertingly spontaneous."

I'm definitely spontaneous, but I'm not very warm and affectionate.

"Attention span in relationships can be short; ENFP's are easily intrigued and distracted by new friends and acquaintances, forgetting about the older ones for long stretches at a time."

I recognize myself in the description. I wonder if Jen is reading this for herself or just for me. I hope she is hearing what she is saying. I want her to know who I am.

"This tells us a lot about how you're wired. You probably don't do well when you're alone, so getting out and making plans with other people is important. Do you have some friends who are supporting you in your recovery?"

Her question reminds me of a worksheet I filled out while I was in treatment.

I'm sitting at a desk in the room I share with a drug addict. I'm filling out mounds of paperwork. I'm thankful to be doing something to kill the time, and filling out forms helps me forget for a moment that I'm in a treatment facility. One of the questions on the form asks me if I have any friends I can count on for support. There are four blank spaces. Next to the questionnaire my elbow is resting on a folded sheet of paper my friend, Nancy, gave me on visitor's day. It's a list of all the people I know who would like to be of some kind of help while I'm in treatment. The list of people fills up one whole side of the paper and spills onto the other. Tears run down my cheeks as I read all the names.

"I have a lot of friends helping me."

"How is JB doing with all of this?"

I look out the window. I haven't even thought about his perspective.

"I don't know. I think he was pretty shocked at first. I hid my drinking pretty well."

"So, you were a closet drinker?"

"More of a laundry room drinker. JB has always worked a lot of weird hours, so I drank mostly while he was away. I tried not to drink too much in case one of the kids got sick or there was an emergency and I had to drive."

I think about how careful I tried to be when I was drinking. I always hid my alcohol well. If I poured a glass of wine, I hid the bottle and then washed out the glass right away. I worried I might drink too much and forget to hide the bottle. One instance in particular stands out, but I'm too embarrassed to tell her the story, especially since I can't remember all of it.

I pour my second glass of Bailey's and vodka over ice. There's a lot more vodka than Bailey's. I'm at the computer writing when the buzz hits me. I feel warm all over. I close my eyes and tip my head back. It feels so good. My head is swimming. Everything slows down. My muscles let go of the tension they've built up since my last drink. I could stay right here forever. I open my eyes and stare at the computer screen. I need to think about what I'm writing. I take another drink. I can't focus anymore so I let it go. I stand up and grab my drink. I walk into the kitchen. I put the glass down and my attention sways from one thing to another like leaves blowing in the wind. I force myself to focus for a moment because I realize I have to wash the glass before I'm too far gone to remember. I look at the glass on the counter. I am fading fast. I need to do something. I just can't think of what it is. Oh, I need to wash out the glass. I take one last drink and the ice cubes hit my nose. I turn and look at the sink. I'm tempted to eat the ice cubes because I'm sure they absorbed some of the alcohol, but I have to get this stuff put away before I can't think anymore. I pour out the ice cubes and stare into the sink. I'm still staring. I look at the glass. I need to wash the glass. I turn on the water. I put soap in the glass and swish it around. I rinse the glass. I dry it out and put it in the cupboard. I look around the kitchen to make sure I didn't leave anything out. I have to hurry because my head is getting heavier and I can't see very clearly. I can barely think now. I need to go to bed. I walk slowly toward the stairs. I drank too much. I get up the stairs and look around. What if the kids wake up? I want to peek in their bedrooms, but I'm not sure I'll make it to bed. I walk into my bedroom and flop onto the bed. My eyes close. The room is spinning. I feel like I'm somewhere else. I love it there.

I open my eyes. My stomach hurts. I don't know how long I've been asleep. I move, and my head feels like a throbbing lead weight. I'm still in my clothes lying on top of my covers. Suddenly, I realize I have to run to the bathroom. I get to the toilet just in time to throw up. Shooting pains rip through my head, and the room is still spinning. What am I doing?! I slide back off my knees and lean against the wall. I try not to move. People don't throw up in the morning from a hangover! Especially not moms! Crap! My kids! I wonder if they're up yet. I wonder what time it is. I have to teach them school today. My stomach starts to roll again as I attempt to get up off the floor. As I walk toward the steps I can hear the TV on. Andy and Johnny are sitting together on the couch watching Sponge Bob. I squint as I go down the stairs and into the kitchen. I put Pop Tarts into the toaster and take some ibuprofen. I tell them I don't feel well so we won't be having school today. I put the Pop Tarts on the table and walk slowly back up the stairs. I lay down on my bed moaning and wishing; wishing I could quit making the same mistake over and over.

"So, what happened that made you quit?"

My last drink is firmly planted in my memory.

"I knew I had a problem, and I kept trying to quit. At one point I had made it almost a year without drinking. Then, the week after Christmas I started again. I don't know why. Before this long stretch, I had only drank at night after the kids went to bed, but this time I started putting Bailey's and vodka in my coffee in the morning and drinking it until noon. Then I switched to wine and drank that the rest of the day. I only did that for a week before I got caught."

"How did you get caught?"

"It was Monday after Christmas break, and I had run out of wine. I was supposed to be teaching my kids, but all I could think about was another drink. So I called another homeschooling friend, told her I was sick, and dropped my kids off at her house."

I stop talking. The memory brings with it a jolt of guilt and shame, and my heart feels like someone stabbed it with a knife. I fight to push the emotions away as I remember what I did next.

I'm standing in the driveway of my friend's house. The kids get out of the van, and I look at each of them slowly. I'm desperate to get to the liquor store, but I need to hold them. They know this house as well as they know our own house but leaving them is different this time. I don't know where I'm going, and I don't know when I'll be back. I look into their eyes. Even at the young age of nine, I can tell that Andy has many of his dad's qualities. He's kind, warm, sensitive and tells me the truth even if he's going to get into trouble. He looks just like his dad too. Jenna is more like me. Her first sentence was, "Do it myself!" We had to get her a toddler bed when she was 18 months old because she could pull herself up over the bars of her crib. Johnny is a combination of both of us. He's gentle and cuddly but on occasion goes into wild fits of anger. Instinctively, I hold him tightly when he's angry until the fight leaves him and he collapses into my arms.

They're anxious to get into the house and see their friends. I hug them longer than usual as I say goodbye. I don't want to leave them here, but everything in me is screaming for a drink. I need alcohol more than I need air.

I take a deep breath as I try to control the emotions that are attempting to escape.

"I picked up a bottle of wine and started drinking as soon as I got home. My friend, Shelly, called because she was coming over for lunch. I totally forgot she was coming, so I told her I didn't feel well, and we'd have to reschedule. Somehow she knew something was wrong. My depression had started a few months before that, so she was worried about me. She knew I had been trying to quit drinking, so she decided she was going to come over and check up on me. I didn't want to lose my new bottle of wine, so I drank the whole thing before she got there, which only took about ten minutes. When she arrived and found me with an empty bottle, she didn't know what to do so she called our friend, Nancy, who is my church's Women's Ministry leader. Nancy is a mentor as well as a friend to both of us. Nancy realized this was more than a little slip up for me, so she called our pastor and our pastor picked up JB from work. It sort of turned out to be a mini, impromptu intervention."

"And then what happened?"

"I was pretty drunk, so I don't remember everything, but at one point everyone was quiet and I couldn't stand the tension anymore, so I joked that I'd never been drunk in front of a pastor before. That didn't go over as well as I hoped it would. I remember JB wanted our kids to spend the night at their friend's house while we sorted things out, but I felt so guilty about leaving them. I needed them to come back home. I wanted them to sleep in their own beds, but I couldn't let them see me like I was, so Nancy said I could spend the night at her house."

There are so many things I can't remember, but my night at Nancy's house plays in slow motion through my mind.

I'm lying on a bed in the guest bedroom. The house is quiet. Light streams in through the window on my right. I watch the specks of dust floating in the sunlight. My face is like stone. My eyelids are heavy. My body is heavy. It takes too much effort to move, so I stay still. Even my thoughts are heavy. I try not to think. I stare at the dust particles for hours. The sunlight fades. The dust particles disappear. There's a knock at the door. I move my eyes toward the door. Nancy walks in quietly and asks how I'm doing. I don't know what to say. I don't know how I'm doing. I feel like a piece of cement. She asks if I want to come down for dinner. I say I'm not hungry. I haven't eaten much in weeks, and my clothes are falling off. She says I should really eat. I say I'm too tired. She says that tomorrow we'll meet JB at a counseling center. I'm afraid to see JB. Maybe it will be easier with a counselor. I wonder if Nancy will stay there with me. I've gone to her with everything the last few years. She knows me better than I know myself. I've always been able to protect myself by not letting people get too close. I'm not sure how or why I've let her in as far as I have, maybe because her love for me seems so genuine and unconditional. She's always there for me. She tells me the truth when it's hard, she encourages me when life seems overwhelming, and she celebrates all my little victories. I've never had a friend like her. Lately, she's been pushing me to share my thoughts with JB, but I'm afraid to talk to him. I feel like we've grown apart over the years. I don't want to think anymore. I just want to fall asleep on this bed and not wake up, ever.

"The next day we met JB at a counselor's office. The counselor realized immediately that I needed a chemical dependency assessment, so she called a treatment center and I was admitted a couple of days later."

"So, how would you describe your marriage right now?"

I look outside the window as I think. It's so hard to think. It's hard to take apart the jumbled thoughts in my head and unscramble them to make a sentence. I see words like trapped, and miserable, and family, and responsibility. I want to leave, but I don't want to hurt my kids.

"I wish it was better."

"How so?"

"I wish we were happy. I wish we had more in common. I wish he helped more with the kids. I wish I could talk to him."

"Why do you think you can't talk to him?"

"I have a hard time putting my thoughts into words. When I do finally find some words to say, he is already way ahead of me and I can't catch up. It makes me feel really stupid and then I just quit talking."

"How long have you been married?"

"Fourteen years."

"Have you always had a hard time talking to JB?"

"No. We used to talk."

I think back to the hours we spent talking in his car when we were young. He used to drop me off at home after youth group. I was eighteen, and he was twenty-six. He was the first person in my life I felt comfortable talking to. We talked for hours about everything.

"We talked a lot when we were younger."

"When do you think that changed?"

I start fast forwarding through my memories from high school to college. I had left home for St. Mary's College in Winona, Minn., two-and-a-half hours away. I said goodbye to JB thinking I might not see him again. I was planning to meet a school full of guys my age, but I couldn't get JB out of my head. None of the guys at school measured up to my expectations. I left school after my sophomore year and married JB when I was twenty-one. He was twenty-nine. We had Andy three years later, Jenna twenty-two months later and Johnny another twenty-two months later. Life was chaos with three little kids.

"JB worked 24-hour shifts, so our schedules clashed, but that was fine before we had kids. There was always time for each other. But after our kids were born, everything was different."

"Kids can do that."

"I don't know what happened between then and now. I just know I can't talk to him like I used to."

She jots something down in her notebook.

"How are your kids? You mentioned you were homeschooling them, and now they are in public school for the first time, right?"

Every time my kids come up my stomach feels like someone is wringing it like a towel, squeezing every last drop of dignity out of my system. Their first day of school comes to mind.

I'm at the treatment center. I've been here since Friday night, but there's no real programming over the weekend, so I've been sitting around filling out paperwork, doing chores, and getting to know the other patients. It's Monday and they wake us up for chores and breakfast. I think of my kids. JB is getting them dressed for their first day of school. It's January and all the kids returned from Christmas break last week. Tears run down my face. I want to run out of the hospital and go home. I want to hug them goodbye before they get on the bus. I want to tell them it will be okay. I want to know what their faces look like. They've never been to a school before. Do they wonder what happened to me? Do they think I abandoned them? Did JB fix them breakfast? I wonder what he put in their lunches. My heart hurts so bad I think it's going to explode.

I always thought they might go to school someday, maybe in Junior High. I always imagined if we sent them to school that it would be a gradual process and we'd talk to them and help them get ready for a classroom setting and go out together with them to buy school supplies and backpacks. Now they are being jolted into a new routine without me there. Andy is smart and independent. He does his work without my nagging him. I wonder if he'll be alright following the school schedule. Jenna never sits still. I let her doodle and walk around while I read because she doesn't hear me when I make her sit still. Johnny loves being with his older siblings. I wonder how he is going to do without them.

I get up from my bed and go into the bathroom. None of the doors lock in this place, so I shut it tightly. I look into the mirror. My reflection is hard to see because the mirror is made of plastic so I can't hurt myself. I can't stop thinking about my kids. I have to think in order to breathe. I can't push back the pain any longer. I fall on my knees and start crying. My shoulders are shaking. Then my whole body is shaking. My sobbing sounds like moaning, and I wonder if someone is going to come find me, but no one does. It's such an unfamiliar sound that I feel like I'm listening to someone else cry. It hurts in the deepest part of me, and the crying doesn't make it feel any better.

I don't know how long it's been. My body is tired and I can't open my eyes. I finally get up off the floor and look in the mirror again. I can't tell the difference. I wash my face with cold water and walk out of the bathroom.

Everyone is in the lounge eating breakfast. No one else knows I'm missing my kids' first day of school.

"They seem fine, but it's hard to tell what they know and what they feel. They seem to be getting used to going to school. Their teachers are really nice and a couple of people from our church work at their school and are keeping an eye on them."

"And what else are you doing in your recovery? Is your treatment done?"

"My inpatient treatment was only for a week. I still have four months of outpatient treatment."

"Is that every day?"

"It's three times a week for a while, then two times a week, and at the end it's one time a week."

"That's great. Where are you going for outpatient treatment?"

"It's at the hospital downtown. My friends are taking turns driving me there."

"Did you lose your license?"

"No. But I wasn't very functional when I got home from treatment. I think they were worried I wouldn't make it to the treatment center without stopping at the liquor store if I drove alone."

"Your cravings are that strong?"

27

Her question takes me to a turning point at the treatment center.

I'm lying in bed, and I can't get to sleep. So many thoughts are rushing around in my head: my family, my friends, lectures, group therapy, the bipolar girl, videos on meth and cocaine, and the physiology of the addict's brain. I'm an alcoholic. I've finally admitted it, and it still seems surreal. I'm tired and humiliated, and I can't imagine ever taking another drink again. How could I do this to my kids? I will never put them through this again! And then it happens. A craving washes over me. It feels like warm honey running through my blood. My mouth waters. I want a drink so bad I can taste it. Fear overwhelms me. I attempt to push the craving away, but it's too strong. I know if there was a way I could have a drink right now, I'd do anything to get it. I'm terrified. What do I do now? How will I ever quit?

"My cravings come and go. Some days they are stronger than I am."

Session 3

I'm in the van driving to my therapy session. I think through my week because I know Jen will ask me about it. Andy came home from school with a poster he made in class. They talked about drugs and alcohol. What a coincidence. Andy's poster has a big wine bottle cut out and glued in the middle. An arrow points from the wine bottle to a stick person with their tongue hanging out. The stick person is standing next to a tombstone. It reads, "When you drink, you can't think." I wonder if Andy is able to connect his school lesson with my hospital stay. It is hard to know what the kids understand. JB told me that while I was gone, he and the kids watched the movie, *Finding Nemo*. In the movie the sharks are trying to quit eating fish so they have a support group meeting and share how long each of them has gone without eating any fish. JB told the kids that I was like the sharks. I'm not sure that was a good idea.

I'm anxious as usual. I'm coming up to a stoplight. I feel a sudden pull to turn right toward the liquor store. To the left is Jen's office. It is all I can do not to swerve into the right turn lane and pull into the liquor store parking lot. I pick up a CD case from the floor and read the Bible verse I taped to it.

"There is now no condemnation for those in Christ Jesus, and because you belong to him, the power of the life-giving Spirit has freed you from the power of sin that leads to death." (Romans 8:1)

I printed out a bunch of Bible verses and taped them to things that I can see while I'm driving. I had a really weird experience with a Bible verse once while I was trying to quit drinking.

I'm holding a bottle of wine. I know I'm drinking too much and I know I need to quit. I keep going through cycles. I drink too much, I'm determined to quit, I go a few days or weeks, the cravings come back and I crumble and buy another bottle. I drink again until my resolve comes back or I do something really stupid. I'm attempting to dump a bottle of wine down the drain again. The fight inside my mind is exhausting. My mouth is watering. I need a drink. I tell myself this is stupid. I need to pour it out. I feel strong until I smell the alcohol, and my resolve melts away in an instant. I set the bottle on the counter and think about getting a glass. The other side of me won't quit. I have to dump out the bottle. I twist my arm to pour it out, but I can't get myself to tip it all the way. I hold it sideways over the sink like a suicidal person climbing onto the ledge, but at the thought of actually pouring it out I panic at the possibility of being in the house without alcohol. My arm is getting tired of holding the bottle sideways. The mental fight has worn me out, and I climb back off the ledge defeated and put the bottle back down on the counter.

I sit on the floor with my head in my arms. I'm such a failure. I tell God I can't do it. I don't want to let him down, but I can't do it. A thought flickers through my head like a voice that's not my own. It says, "I don't expect you to do this. I will do it, but you have to let me."

Then a short Bible verse comes to mind and I say it out loud. "I can do all things through Christ who strengthens me." (Philippians 4:13) I say it again as I stand up by the sink. "I can do all things through Christ who strengthens me."

I pick up the bottle as I continue to repeat the verse. I'm aware that I'm about to dump the very thing I'm desperate for, but I keep repeating the verse. It's like magic. Effortlessly, I pour the wine down the drain. Part of me watches in disbelief. My hand that's dumping the bottle doesn't feel like it belongs to me. The last drops spill out, and I set the bottle on the counter and stare at it. It's like someone else was dumping the bottle. I'm kind of freaked out.

Now there are Bible verses all over my car; on my CD covers, the sun visor, the steering wheel and half the speedometer. Any time the craving for alcohol washes over me, I read one of the verses out loud to get rid of the thought.

I'm in the left hand turn lane, and I read this verse over and over until the liquor store is out of sight. It's never quite out of mind.

I pull into the parking lot of Jen's office, turn off the engine and sit. I'm a few minutes early. I draw a deep breath and get out of the car. I open the front door of the office building and walk straight to the bathroom. It's becoming a ritual. Everything is in slow motion. There's an overpowering floral smell from the soap. My hands are dry, and I don't have any lotion. I look in the mirror. I don't know the person staring back at me. I look at my watch. I need to get to the office. I open the heavy bathroom door and start down the long, narrow hallway. I hope I don't see anyone. There's always a door or two open along the way. People are sitting around a table talking. Another door opens to some people carrying food. I try not to make eye contact with anyone. I get to the office door and take another deep breath before I turn the knob. The doorbell noise alerts Jen that I'm there, and I hear her voice calling from her office.

"Come in."

I walk past the play room and the other two office doors. They're both empty. There are magazines on the coffee table in the waiting room where there is a couch and two chairs. I walk in.

I sit on the couch and sink down. I hate this couch. I feel like it swallows me every time I sit on it. Jen sits in her chair across from me. I wonder about her. She's not what I expected a Christian counselor to be like. I'm not sure what I was expecting, but she seems to share some of my rebellious nature. She doesn't fit my stereotypical image of Christianity; firm, serious, slightly condescending. Jen is gentle, kind, and nonjudgmental.

"How was your week?"

I think for a moment.

"I went to a Women's Expo at our church. They offered different classes. I didn't really want to go, but I thought it would be good to get out with people."

"Great! How did it go?"

"It was good and bad. I signed up for two classes. My first one was a drawing class. It was really relaxing."

My shoulders droop and my back sinks into the cushions as I think back to that morning.

I'm sitting at a table, and the sun is coming in the window. I'm surrounded by familiar faces. It's comforting and upsetting at the same time. I've made so many close friends and memories at this church that just being here feels good, but I'm assuming everyone now knows I'm an alcoholic who went to treatment. I've felt mixed reactions from people. Some have come right out and asked me how I am with concerned looks on their faces. Others have completely ignored me. I'm learning quickly who my friends are.

In this drawing class, we're supposed to be copying this picture but upside down. Right side up, the picture is of a man sitting in a chair. Upside down it's only shapes. My eyes trace the shapes. I find a spot on the paper where I think a shape starts. My hand begins to draw a curved line then a straight line at a little bit of an angle to the curve. I keep drawing what I see until I connect the last line. My anxiety is gone, and my hands aren't shaking. My body is relaxed, and my mind seems clear. I want to draw more, but my picture is done. I turn it right side up, and it looks nearly the same as the original. I smile.

"Then I went to my second class. That didn't go as well."

I'm sitting in the middle of a row of people. I haven't been very talkative, and I hope it starts soon so I don't have to talk to anyone. This class is about organization and is run by two women in our church. One works for a

33

large corporation and the other runs a volunteer organization. They pass around a packet of handouts on organizing ideas. They begin to talk about how they organize their house, their lists, groceries, money, etc. My head starts to hurt. I try to concentrate, but there's so much information. My house is always a mess. I've never been able to get everything in its right place. I thought an organizing class would help me get a good start during my recovery.

While in treatment, I was thankful, but humiliated to find that my friends had come into my house and cleaned. One couple did our heaping pile of laundry. Another cleaned the bathrooms. Many had come over with food and did the dishes. One of JB's best friends went through the house with him looking for hidden wine bottles.

The class continues and I can't sit still. I start tapping my feet on the floor and doodling on my handouts. My heart is beating faster, and I'm getting hot. They begin to talk about putting Post-it notes on the last bottle of shampoo in the closet so when you get to it, you can take the Post-it note off and place it on your shopping list to save time. How does anyone think of that? How do they have time to put Post-it notes on everything? Do people really have two or three of everything stocked in their closets ready to be used when the previous one runs out? I wonder if they're just kidding and the real teaching will come after the sarcasm is over. As they talk, I realize they aren't joking. I imagine myself putting a Post-it note on my deodorant in the closet. I know that even if I remember to take the Post-it note off the deodorant, it will never make it all the way downstairs to my grocery list, if I had a grocery list. When I actually make a list, I don't remember to bring it to the store. I see Post-it notes on my handout. I scratch it off the list.

My head is pounding now, and I'm praying they are done talking. I want to get up and walk out, but I'm in the middle of the row, and I don't want to draw attention to myself. I look around and people are taking notes. I have to get out of here. I heard about panic attacks from one of the guys in treatment, and I feel like I might have one right now. I close my eyes and start thinking about something else. I start thinking about the last time I was here at this event. I was teaching guitar as one of the classes. I didn't know how to play more than four chords, but my friend, Karen was great at playing, so I got her to teach it with me. We ran late because I wasn't keeping track of time and our class was having a lot of fun. That was my favorite thing to do; have fun. I don't remember the last time I had fun.

Finally, the organizing session is over. Everything they didn't cover is on the handouts, so we can read through them later. I just want to get out of this room. I wish I hadn't signed up for this. My head hurts. Every nerve ending that had relaxed during the drawing class is now standing on end like goose bumps.

"The second class was about organizing, and I became extremely anxious."

"Why did you take an organizing class?"

"Because I'm so unorganized. I thought it might be helpful."

"You need to start focusing on your strengths, and quit trying to become good at the things you're not gifted at. Do you remember the personality test you took?"

"Yeah."

"You are a 'P', perceiving. It is not natural for you to be able to organize. You are not gifted administratively, and you need to realize that you will never force yourself to become this kind of person. It is not who God made you to be. You need to begin to see the gifts God gave you and focus on those. It is the only way you will be happy."

That makes sense, but I'm afraid if I don't keep trying to make it perfect, it will end up looking like my mom's house with piles of papers everywhere and dishes left undone and mail unopened and things lost. Jen sits back in her chair, looks through the titles on her bookshelf and pulls one out.

"Have you read this yet?"

"No."

She hands me a book. It's called, *Adult Children of Alcoholics, by* Janet Woititz.

"Adult children of alcoholics often believe they should be able to do everything and that everyone but them has it all together."

Jen gets up and opens her file drawer. I begin to look through the chapter titles of the book and my curiosity piques as I read them. "What Happened to You as a Child?" "What is Happening to You Now?" My eyes go to the first chapter and I open the book to page one and read, "When is a child not a child? When the child lives with alcoholism. But, more correctly, when is a child not childlike? You certainly looked like a child and dressed like a child. Other people saw you as a child, unless they got close enough to see that edge of sadness in your eyes or that worried look on your brow. You behaved much like a child, but you were not really frolicking, you were more just going along. You didn't have the same spontaneity that the other kids had. But no one really noticed that. That is, unless they got very close, and even if they did, they probably didn't understand what it meant."

I want to read more. This author knows me. No one has ever understood what it's like. As a child, it seemed everyone else got to do life together on the playground, and I had to watch from outside the fence. I tried to fit in. I played jump rope even though I didn't like it because all the girls did it. I went to birthday parties and friends' houses, but I never felt like I belonged. I always felt alone. Maybe it was because I didn't feel like I could invite friends over to my house. I did eventually let a friend come over once. That was a mistake.

We get off the bus at my stop. I'm nervous. I wish I hadn't said she could come over. We've been to her house so many times, she was getting bored and wanted to come to my house, but I wouldn't let her. She finally talked me into it. I already told her about my wild brothers and that my mom didn't cook or clean, but I don't think anything I said could really prepare her for what is coming.

We walk up the steep driveway. Bikes are leaning against the garage. A large wooden spool used for the electrical wires by the telephone company sits on its side and is used as a table for piles of old tools, buckets, string, toys, etc. A basketball hoop stands at the edge of the dirt driveway. Behind the hoop is a huge pile of split wood covered by a metal framed truck topper. A large blue tarp covers the topper to keep the wood dry. Beyond the wood pile is a fire pit with big logs as seats. One of the seats around the fire pit is an old van bench which is faded and ripped from being outside. Some old, rusted, metal chairs are scattered here and there.

A clothesline hangs from the garage to the front porch where my mom hangs clean clothes. There's rarely anything on it. The front porch has green outdoor carpet over the concrete steps and landing. My dad is a carpet layer, and all around the outside of the house are large pieces of old carpet he couldn't throw away. Even the path from the house down to the lake is carpeted. I never thought much about it, but seeing it through Carrie's eyes makes it look so weird.

I'm trying to escape somewhere in my mind so I don't have to actually be here as she looks around. I wonder what she's thinking. We go into the house. The entryway is covered with coats and hats and scarves and mittens all hanging on six inch nails that my dad pounded into the wall. A large freezer takes up much of the space and more boxes and coats and stuff that never found a place are piled on the freezer. Carrie starts taking off her shoes. I quickly tell her to leave them on. I'm hoping the floor isn't wet today. When it's wet, your shoes stick as you walk and I don't think I could handle that right now.

We walk through the kitchen where the dirty dishes fill up both sinks, most of the counter and a box on the floor. I suddenly panic that she might want something to drink. I hope there's at least one clean glass in the cupboard. Maybe she won't ask. The kitchen table is hard to see under the piles of cereal boxes, months of unopened mail, a sewing machine, old food, and anything else that may have been set down and lost or forgotten. A bucket sits in the middle of the floor to catch the drips from the crack in the ceiling.

We get through the kitchen to the dining room. In the middle of the room is a table, but we never eat there because it's always piled high with stuff. Sometimes we move a pile onto the floor so we can do homework. All those piles are still surrounding the table. I don't do much homework. If I do any, I do it in my room. More piles cover the small antique desk and the buffet cabinet. In between the piles are knickknacks covered in dust. Pictures of generations of family cover the walls which have yellowed with my dad's cigarette smoke.

My parent's bedroom is off the dining room. The door doesn't quite open or shut all the way because of the clothes on the floor and hanging over the door. My dad doesn't sleep in there anymore. He usually watches TV until he passes out on the couch. The living room is a long, narrow room which we divided in half with old bed sheets. With seven kids and only three bedrooms, we needed a place for the boys to sleep. A large porch is connected to the living room. The back porch is really the front porch because the people who moved the house from its original site put it on backward. The house movers also took a short cut across a frozen pond to avoid the road's sharp turn, and the house went through the ice. My mom has a picture of the house from the newspaper. The first floor was almost all under water. Our front porch, which is now our back porch, is full from floor to ceiling with clothes, games, toys, furniture and stuff. Once we cleaned half of it out so my brothers could move from the living room to the porch but it was only a three season porch and it got too cold in the winter to be out there.

There's a bathroom off the kitchen. It smells all the time. Sometimes the sewer system backs up, and we can't flush anything down the toilet so it goes in the garbage can which no one ever takes out. The cabinet is full of prescription bottles that are half used. My mom keeps them in case we need them again.

I take Carrie upstairs to my bedroom. I feel numb. Carrie tells me she has to use the bathroom. Oh no. I didn't anticipate that. The upstairs bathroom is floor to ceiling pink, from the pink shag carpet to the pink walls and bathtub. The bathtub had become rust colored from our well water so my dad used pink exterior paint to cover the rust. The paint is now coming off in layers, mostly while someone is taking a bath. The water pressure is so low that we barely get our hair washed. I point the way for her and hold my breath. She will probably have to hold hers too. It seems like it's been forever, but Carrie comes out of the bathroom. She doesn't say anything and I don't either.

Carrie and I play in my room for a while. I want to keep her as far away as I can from the rest of the family. I'm also beginning to worry that my dad might come home early. Letting Carrie see my house is scary, but it's not as bad as the fear I feel thinking my dad might come home drunk while she's here. My room has a huge hole in the wall from the time I threw my bowling ball through it.

The screens of the windows have large circular holes in them. My brothers cut the holes so they could lower their action figures down the two stories with ropes. I can't open the window in the summer now without letting in a ton of bugs and we don't have air conditioning.

We play for a while until her mom comes to pick her up. I bring Carrie downstairs to wait because I don't want her mom to come to the door. I really like Carrie's mom. She makes dinner when I'm at her house. We all sit at the table and she makes an excuse about her cooking not being very good, but I love it. Then her dad tells us to clean our plates and put them in the dishwasher. Carrie complains about it, but I always try to do extra. I clear off the rest of the table and wash dishes. Carrie gets mad at me for being so nice to her parents, but I can't help it. They like me and appreciate it when I help. It makes me feel wanted.

As Carrie's mom pulls into the driveway I grab Carrie's bag and run her out to the car. I open the door for Carrie and thank her mom for picking her up. Then I shut the door and walk away fast because I think the faster she leaves the less trash and junk she'll see. Her car pulls out of the driveway, and I watch the dust rise up and settle on their car. I take a deep breath. It's over.

The next day at school I'm nervous to see Carrie, because I don't know how she'll react to me after seeing where I live. I walk down the hall to my locker, and I see her getting her books out of her locker. I bend down and slowly put my things away. She shuts her locker and comes over and starts talking about the softball game tonight and if I finished my homework. I'm relieved she's

41

talking to me.   Neither of us ever mentions my house...ever.

Jen finds the sheet she's looking for in her cabinet and I shut the book. She grabs an erasable marker and draws a few lines on the whiteboard.

"Let's draw out your family tree."

This looks familiar. My mom has made hundreds of family tree charts. Ninety percent of our conversations involve our dead relatives. It's one of her jobs as a Mormon. She needs to find all of our dead relatives so she can put their names in temple rituals so they have the option to become a Mormon in the afterlife. She also keeps two years of food stored in the basement for when Jesus comes back to the earth and everything is chaos. Our food storage was probably not maintained as well as the average Mormon's storage. I remember one time when I was younger it got a little out of control.

My brother and I are walking slowly down the basement steps. It's dark down there, and we've watched every horror movie made even though we are only eight and ten years old. The only light switch that works is the string that hangs from the light bulb in the middle of the basement. There's just enough light to see the outline of the stairs. I make Brian go down first. It takes us forever to go down three stairs because we're both fighting over who goes first. We finally calm ourselves down enough to focus on getting the basement light on. We know once we get the light on the fear will evaporate.

We take a couple more steps and then freeze. We both see the same thing, and we can't move or talk. We are frozen for five long seconds as we try to process what we see. In the shadows there is something about a foot off the ground waving back and forth. We come to our senses and start screaming as we fall over each other trying to get up the stairs. We are still screaming as we rush to tell my dad about the thing in the basement. We usually don't tell him anything for fear he will give us chores to do for the rest of the day, but this is an emergency. My dad sighs and gets up off the couch in the middle of his football game. He starts down the stairs to turn on the light. Brian and I stand behind the door as my dad walks down as if nothing is wrong. We soon hear a string of expletives, but he doesn't sound like he's getting hurt. He just sounds mad. We hear the light click on and we can't help ourselves from peeking, even if we might witness the scene from a horror movie. My dad is standing in the middle of the basement surrounded by knee high brown looking grass. It turns out one of my mom's barrels of wheat had broken open and spread into the carpet. Our basement floods sometimes, and it must have been damp enough for the wheat to grow. My brother and I sit on the steps fascinated by the National Geographic scene right in our very own basement.

Jen writes my name on the middle of the board.

"What's your dad's name?"

"Jack."

She writes down Jack.

"What's your mom's name?"

"Sarah."

"How many siblings do you have?"

"Six."

She puts all the family members on the board.

"How many people are in your dad's family?"

I start thinking about my dad's family. They were definitely not Mormon. Their God was beer, and they religiously played poker. In my mind my dad's family is synonymous with Cumberland, Wis., where my aunt and uncle live. We spent every holiday there for as long as I can remember. Our gatherings might not have been like the traditional family, but it was what I knew and the thought of it makes me smile.

Grandma is sitting on the couch with her brother, Butch. They've both been drinking beer all day setting the bar high for the rest of the family. They're laughing as they tell stories. They both have long noses and sharp cheek bones. They're Bohemian. My dad calls us Bo-hunks. He says that's where we get our spit and vinegar. We try not to get too close or we'll end up having to get grandma another beer or listen to a long, boring story or both.

My cousins and I play outside all day. They have a jeep and dirt bikes that we take back into the woods. They let us ride the dirt bikes, but not as much as I'd like, and I want one so bad I can't stand it. There's a pond where we skate in the winter and canoe in the summer. Mostly we play games in the woods. My aunts make the best food and dinnertime is a feast. Before I'd had one of my aunt's burgers, I didn't know they were supposed to be so big

44

and juicy. My dad doesn't want us to get sick from raw meat, so our burgers look like Kingsford charcoal briquettes. These family gatherings are one of the few times my family eats together.

After dinner our parents stay up late playing poker in my uncle's shop. He does upholstery, and his shop is connected to the kitchen. We get chased out of the room several times, but I keep coming back to watch. I love the smell of the cigarette smoke and the warmth of everyone sitting together and laughing. They play until early in the morning. By then, all of us kids have fallen asleep somewhere around the house. When we wake up in the morning we walk over relatives who have passed out on the floor and head outside for another day of fun.

"My dad has two older sisters, two younger brothers and his mom and dad are both dead."

"How about your mom?"

I have to think harder about my mom's side because we never see them. They live on the east coast and the west coast. The last time I saw them was a family reunion in Myrtle Beach when I was twelve years old. My mom drove us out there by herself. We didn't have the money to stay in a hotel so she slept at the rest stops while I watched my brothers. It was fun to see the ocean, but we didn't feel very welcomed, which made more sense later when I found out my mom ran off with my dad, and my mom's relationship with her stepmom was already pretty strained before leaving.

"My mom has four brothers and one sister."

Jen writes these on the board.

"Two of her brothers are half-brothers, and her sister is adopted."

"So, she comes from a blended family."

"Yeah."

Jen makes x's and o's for my mom's family, then turns to me.

"Ok, how many of these relatives have a problem with alcohol?"

That's the first easy question she's asked me.

"All of my dad's family."

Jen puts a big circle around my dad and each of his siblings.

"How about your grandparents?"

"My grandpa died before I was born, but my dad said he drank a lot."

Between my mom's and dad's stories, I have a picture of what my grandparents' lives were like. His dad sounded pretty violent, and his mom might have had some mental health problems. Schizophrenia came up once, but I don't really know for sure. It's hard to tell what someone is like when they are drunk all the time.

"I had never seen my grandma without a beer and cigarette in her hand. And I've only seen my mom's parents once when I was twelve."

"You mean your other grandparents?"

"Well, my grandmother is really a step grandmother, and from what I've heard my mom didn't get along with her very well. My mom's parents don't really feel like grandparents. At least they don't fit my image of a grandparent."

I wonder what it would have been like to have a grandparent's house to escape to where there were warm cookies and cold milk and someone who had time to sit still and patiently listen even if I didn't know what to say.

Jen is quiet. She's looking at the whiteboard. I feel compelled to tell her more.

"I was named after my real grandmother who died when my mom was ten. My mom didn't want to upset her stepmother, so instead of naming me Virginia and calling me Ginny, like her mom, she named me Jennifer so she could call me Jenny, which was as close as she could get."

I pause for a moment. It's the first time I've said that out loud and it sounds so bizarre.

"My mom told me once when I was twelve that she wished I was her mom and she could be my daughter because I was so mature and responsible and talented like her mom. She always compared me to her mom. It always felt like she wanted me to become her mom."

47

"So, you really didn't have a mom."

I look down at the floor. There's a long silence. The reality of her statement cuts me so deeply I can't breathe. If I could bleed emotional pain, the floor would be covered in it. I can't talk, so Jen does.

"Children with alcoholic parents often parent their own parents as well as their siblings."

Thinking about my siblings sends a surge of adrenaline through me. My passion for them feels a lot like the passion I have for my own kids, so the weight I feel about being a bad parent is compounded when I think of how badly I parented my brothers and sisters. My sense of guilt is huge, and I suddenly need to tell Jen about it to get it off my shoulders.

"I tried to take care of my brothers and sisters, but I wasn't very good at it. I was a terrible cook, and I never knew where to start when it came to cleaning the house."

My mind flashes back to when I was twelve and trying to make spaghetti.

I'm standing at the stove. I washed a pan and put water in it and put it on the stove. I dump the noodles into the cold water. While they're cooking I wash some plates and forks and clear a spot at the table. When I think the noodles have probably cooked long enough, I strain them and put the spaghetti on the table. I yell for the boys to come eat. The phone rings and I answer it. It's one of my friends. My brothers are making a lot of noise while I'm trying to talk on the phone. Just as I turn to yell at them to shut up, a huge wad of spaghetti hits me in the face. They couldn't have planned the timing any better. My jaw clenches, and my heart is racing. I want to explode as I put the phone down, but I see the look of terror on their faces. As soon as they see me pause, their frightened faces turn to smiles, and they burst out laughing. I'm trying not to laugh because I'm fuming, but I can't help it. Normally this would set me off into a rage, but luckily for them, I get caught up in the laughter this time.

"I also had a really bad temper."

I never thought of it before, but now that I'm in a therapist's office I wonder if what I did would be called abuse. I don't think I can get into legal trouble though if I was only twelve years old. Every episode was the same.

Ben and Sam are fighting in the living room. I yell at them to stop. Of course, they don't stop. It's over some dumb toy. They are rolling on top of each other, and I yell at them again. They act like they didn't hear a word I said which makes my body temperature rise from the inside out. Sam starts crying because Ben went too far, again. I explode in a rage and run toward him. He's scared, and before I can stop myself I punch him in the leg, and he starts crying. Crap! Why did I do that? Now I'm furious with myself. I turn and run up the stairs into the hallway where a full length mirror hangs on the wall. I look at myself, and I'm so disgusted I start pounding on the wall with my fists. Why can't I control myself?! I hate myself! I hate my life! My hand goes through the thin sheet of drywall, but I don't feel any pain. I stomp into my bedroom and slam the door. I fall onto my bed crying, wishing I could be a better sister to them. As my anger dissolves, my hand is starts to hurt where I pounded it through the wall.

"I watched my siblings enough that they called me mom, but I didn't do a very good job."

"Your siblings called you mom?"

Jen seems surprised by this which makes me uncomfortable because she rarely looks surprised, and I assume she's heard worse stories than mine. I try to read her face when I answer.

"Yeah, but they always corrected themselves, like they would yell, 'Mom! ... I mean, Jenny!' You know, so it's not like they really thought I was their mom. It was just kind of a habit for them I guess."

Jen's eyes soften. It's hard to believe they can get softer than they already are. My heart melts a little bit each time she does it.

"Do you know that as a child, you shouldn't have had to be a parent to your siblings?"

"Yeah, but I still feel bad that I didn't do it very well."

"But it wasn't your job."

"I know, but I couldn't just ignore them."

"Just because your parents didn't do their job, doesn't mean that you should have had to do their job."

"But I was there. If I didn't do it, then it wouldn't get done. It didn't get done anyway, but I really tried the best I could."

50

Guilt wells up inside my chest, and I feel tears coming. I clench my jaw and push them back. I should have been a better sister. I should have been able to make them do their chores and eat meals and get them to bed on time. I should have been able to keep them from fighting all the time. I should have been able to keep them from hurting themselves like they did. I should have stayed home instead of leaving for college. I hang my head and I can't look up. If I couldn't do it then, why did I think I could do it now with my own kids? Why did I even have kids? Now they are stuck with me! If I could, I would wish them into a different home with a mom who could clean and cook and get them to bed on time and read stories every night and keep her voice calm. They would have structure and love and not chaos and pain.

"Jenny, this was your parents' ball to drop and not your ball to pick up. As a child, you couldn't have been their parent no matter how hard you tried. Children are not capable of parenting other children."

I think about how I failed my siblings and my nightmares come to mind. Maybe she'll understand how I felt if I tell her about them. I need to explain how responsible I felt. I hold my breath as I let the pictures sink into my consciousness.

"I had nightmares for years while we were growing up. I always had to save my brothers and sisters from some life-threatening situation. One time they were in a barn that was on fire. Sometimes they were in a van that was sinking into a lake, but most of the time we were being chased by a man. No matter how many times I killed the man, he kept coming back to life."

51

There's one dream in particular that was worse than all the others. I can't get it out of my head, but it's so gruesome I don't know if I want to tell Jen about it.

I'm in a glass house with my brothers and sisters. The house is surrounded by trees. The lights are on, so the man who is chasing us can see inside but we can't see out. I hurry the kids down the stairs into the basement. I take a knife off the counter and stand by the basement stairs guarding them. Then the man is in the house. I can feel it. I'm trembling. Then he's there, right in front of me. I stab him, but he doesn't die. He never dies. I keep stabbing him. He falls to the floor. He looks dead, but he always comes back to life. I know he's going to come back to life, and I'm panicking because I'm so tired of being afraid of him. I can't let him come back to life this time. I have to do something. I start cutting him into pieces because I think that maybe if he is in pieces he can't come back to life. I can feel the knife cutting through his flesh. It's so gross, but I'm crazy now. I have to do it. There's no other choice. I put all the pieces into bags. I tie up the bags and bury them in holes far apart from each other. Even after they're buried, I'm still afraid that the pieces will come back together somehow. I feel like I will never completely be rid of him.

"What do you think the man represented in your dream? Was there something that threatened your safety?"

The dreams felt so real. I was always so relieved when I woke up and realized it was just another dream. I think for a moment about her question. I was never physically abused. I was just scared a lot.

"Well, a lot of times when my dad was drunk, he would yell and scream at my mom. I never saw him hit her, but he threw things and broke things and a lot of times he threatened her by saying that if she didn't start cleaning our house he was going to call social services, and they would come and take us all away."

My heart pounds harder thinking about it. My greatest fear growing up was the thought that at any moment someone could show up at our house and take us all away.

I'm twelve and in my bedroom wondering if our tree fort is big enough for our temporary hiding place in case strangers show up at our house to take us away. Nobody will adopt all of us. They'll split us up for sure. The fort is not very big, and the tree is hard to climb. I don't know if I can get my baby sister up there. Even if I could, it's probably not safe. There's also the old shack down by the lake. It's pretty gross, but I don't think anyone would look for us there. I would have to cover the hole in the floor, but there's extra wood. Once I found a job, we could move into an apartment. I wonder how old I have to be to get a job. I don't know if my brother can handle babysitting while I'm gone. I don't even know how I'm going to get everyone out of the house. I have to figure out a plan because I will never let anyone split us apart. My head spins trying to come up with a plan. I finally drift off to another restless night's sleep.

"That would explain why there was always a bad guy after you in your dreams."

"Yeah, I guess it would."

Session 4

Jen and I are back in the play therapy room sitting at the table with the sand tray, except instead of putting action figures in the sand, Jen sets down a piece of paper in front of me and some markers.

"I want you to draw a picture of how you feel."

"Ok."

I look at the markers. I don't know what to draw, but it's easier to draw than talk. The black and the red markers stand out to me. I pick up the black marker and place the tip on the paper. I quit trying to think and I just draw. I make some peaks on a mountain. Then I draw another mountain on the other side of the paper and a valley in the middle. I draw myself as a stick person on the top of the mountain and a huge boulder hanging on the edge. I don't have to try to think anymore. It's just coming. I make a frown and angry eyebrows and my arms on the boulder because I'm pushing the boulder off the cliff. I look at the valley and then at the markers. I choose light colors and draw three stick people in the valley; one light blue, one orange and the smallest one yellow. I put the light colors down and pick up the black marker again and draw stairs going up the side of the mountain. Then I draw a box around myself with bars on it. I make the boulder so it's just barely hanging, about to fall down on top of the three stick figures in the valley. I look at the picture, put the marker down and look up at Jen.

"Who is at the top of the mountain?"

"That's me."

"Why are you in a cage?"

"I feel trapped."

"Who are the three people in the valley?"

"Those are my kids."

"And what are you doing with the boulder?"

"I'm pushing it over the cliff on top of them."

"Why?"

"I don't want to, but I don't know how to stop."

"What do you think the boulder represents?"

I look at my little stick figure children in the valley and think about Andy.

We're in the neurologist's office. She is helping us determine why Andy has a facial twitch. Our pediatrician said most kids grow out of them, but he hasn't. I'm trying not to think about the worst, but thoughts of brain tumors and cancer creep into my mind. She checks Andy's reflexes. Then she makes him follow her fingers with his eyes as she moves them up and down, back and forth. She gives him a few more instructions and then tells us he's fine. JB and I look at her. I don't know what to say. She hasn't done any scans or anything. She just moved her fingers around! She tells us to take him to an eye doctor and a psychologist. I can't move. She's staring at us. Andy hops off the table and walks toward me. I still can't talk. I want her to do something. JB says something and I follow him out of the office holding Andy's hand. I start thinking about who we're going to call next. Obviously, she doesn't know what she's talking about. I can't believe we're going to pay for this.

We decide to take him to the eye doctor and psychologist so we can check that off our list before we find a competent neurologist. Then we can show that we followed her orders. The eye doctor says Andy has a slight stigmatism, but it's not enough to cause twitching. We get him some glasses anyway. Then we take him to a child psychologist at a nearby counseling center. We explain to her briefly what has happened with his twitching. She asks to have a few minutes alone with Andy. We sit in the waiting room. Two large pictures of flower arrangements are hanging just above the cherry wood trim. One frame is slightly crooked, and I want to get up and straighten it, but there are people sitting in front of it. Several minutes later, Samantha comes out of her office. She tells us she is really glad we brought him. He is showing some signs that could be causing his twitching. I can't move again. I can't talk. She asks for a few more minutes with him. I look around the office and begin to wonder what she saw. Maybe my drinking and anger have caused his twitching. My heart suddenly feels like lead. I slump into a chair. My mind is trying to wander back through his young life, but I can't think. I stare at the crooked picture frame. The people who were sitting in front of the picture are gone, and there's no one else in the waiting room, so I get up and push the bottom edge of the frame until it's straight.

"Andy is in play therapy. He has a twitch, and I think it's because of me. I yell a lot. It's like it comes out of nowhere. One minute they make a mess and I'm fine, and the next minute Jenna spills some milk and I completely explode."

I see pictures in my head of things I've done. I look at the floor. I like Jen so much; I don't want to tell her things that will make her think less of me. But, I have to tell her. My kids are more important. I take a deep breath.

"One time when Jenna was three years old, I exploded and was screaming at her. I didn't stop until I saw the look on her face. She was terrified. I knew then that I needed help. I worried that next time…"

I trail off. I don't want to think about it.

"Next time what?"

I close my eyes.

"Next time…I might hit her."

I open my eyes and look beyond Jen to a picture on the wall. I can still see my daughter's face. She is curled up in a ball. Her eyes are so big. People used to stop me on the street to say what beautiful, big eyes she had. Now they are full of terror. I want so much to disappear, to make everything I've done go away. I am the person I swore I would never become. I hate myself.

"I also spanked Johnny once. I mean, I had spanked him before, but one time I did it too hard. I was out of control."

I stop talking and put my head down. I close my eyes. After I did it, I knew I had crossed the line. It was as if someone else was in my body.

Johnny is screaming and holding his bottom. My heart falls down through my chest. I am frozen. If I could die right now I would. I pick him up and sit in the rocking chair. I rock him back and forth and back and forth. His crying finally dies down. I hold him tight. Tears run down my cheeks. I want to say I'm sorry, but he's so little. He doesn't understand. He's so sweet and innocent. He deserves better than me. He stops crying and falls asleep in my arms, but I'm not done rocking him. I'm still crying.

"It might seem like your anger erupts without any warning, but there are signs you can watch for and ways to keep yourself from exploding."

Jen gets up and opens a desk drawer. She flips through some files and pulls out a piece of paper. I think about child abuse. Before I had kids I wondered how someone could hurt their own child. I don't wonder anymore. I love my children more than anything. If someone else tried to hurt them, I'd kill them. So, how do I hurt the people I love the most?

"This is a chain analysis chart. It will take us step by step through a situation and help us see where your anger comes from, and it will help you figure out what thoughts you need to change in order to change your behavior."

I look at the worksheet as Jen walks me through it.

"What is something that just happened this week that you see as a problem behavior?"

It doesn't take me long to think of being angry.

"I blew up yesterday and threw a baseball bat across the garage."

"Ok, write that in the first blank where it says problem behavior.'"

I write in "angry" and "threw a bat in the garage."

"Ok, what was the prompting event that started you on this chain to the problem behavior?"

"What do you mean?"

"What happened right before you blew up?"

"Nothing."

"Something happened. It doesn't matter what it was. It could be anything."

"Well, I think I was making dinner."

"Ok, write that down."

I write down making dinner in the box entitled, "Prompting Event."

"Do you remember how you were feeling while you were making dinner?"

"I think I was frustrated."

"Do you remember why you were frustrated?"

"Because I was making a frozen pizza."

"Was there something frustrating about that?"

"If I was a good mom, I'd be making something other than frozen pizza."

"What would a good mom do?"

"She'd make a healthy meal with vegetables and fruit. She'd make sure they have all their food groups and nutrition and they'd eat together and everyone would do their part, helping to set and clear the table. It would be like the *Brady Bunch*."

"Do you think there are real families like the *Brady Bunch*?"

"Yes."

I don't know why she'd ask that. Isn't everyone's family like the *Brady Bunch*? That's all I want. If I could be a combination of Mrs. Brady and Caroline Ingalls from *Little House on the Prairie*, I'd be perfect and my kids would be perfect and life would be perfect.

"One of the myths adult children of alcoholics believe is that everyone's family looks like the families on TV. Actually, most families are dysfunctional in one way or another."

I think about one of my mom's friends. Her house is spotless and her kids are perfect. Once, her son didn't make his bed before he left for school, so she went to the school, picked him up and brought him home to make his bed. My mom was appalled that her friend would do something like that over an unmade bed. I thought it was a little overboard, but it worked. It intrigued me. I wondered if that's what you had to do to keep order in the house.

"What else was going on that day before you began to make dinner?"

"I ran some errands in the morning, and I was meeting someone in the afternoon, so I didn't have time to go running."

"Do you feel better after you run?"

"Yes."

I think about how running has always been an outlet for me. When I'm really frustrated, JB carefully asks me if I want to go for a run. I get mad at him every time he asks because I know he's really just saying I'm crabby. But when I get back from running I feel like a different person.

"How often do you run?"

"I've been trying to run every day now."

"That's good."

She writes it on her whiteboard.

"Is there anything else you could have changed about your day that would have helped you not explode by dinnertime?"

"I guess if I'd had less things to do I wouldn't have felt so rushed. I would have had time to run. And if I'd planned ahead for dinner, I wouldn't have been late to my meeting."

"And how did all those activities make you feel?"

"I was mad that I had to go to a meeting that night. I was mad that I was an alcoholic. I was mad that JB doesn't trust me, and I was mad that my schedule was so crazy that day."

Jen stands and starts writing the list of things I did that day on the whiteboard.

"So, you didn't run, you had too many things scheduled, you aren't accepting reality and you're beating yourself up. Looking at your environment, what do you think you could do to reduce your vulnerability to anger?"

I look at the whiteboard.

"What do you mean?"

"What are some things you could do that would lessen the chance of you getting angry?"

I start thinking about that day and how uncontrollable it feels when everything inside of me begins to erupt. I had my outpatient group that morning. I ran errands. I had lunch with a friend. By the time I got home I didn't have time to run. I hate it when I can't run. I clench my fist. I breathe and try to think.

"I always feel better when I run."

"Ok, so you know running should be a priority for you."

"Yeah, I guess so."

"What could you have done to fit running into your schedule?"

"I would have had to skip lunch to go running."

"That's good."

She crosses out "lunch" from the whiteboard list. I feel a little weight lifting as I look at the word lunch with a big line through it. I'd never thought of cancelling something like that. What a great idea.

"What else?"

"I could have asked JB to pick up his own dry cleaning. He works really close to the cleaners."

Jen puts a line through "errands" on her whiteboard. As she does, I don't feel any lighter. I feel guilty. I don't ask

JB to do anything because he works and I stay home. I feel like it's my job to do everything else.

"How about dinner? How could that be better?"

"If I had planned ahead, maybe we'd have healthier meals and we could all eat together."

"That's really good. Now, what could you change about the thoughts you were thinking during dinner about being a bad mom?"

"Well…"

I feel like she wants me to say I'm a good mom or at least that I'm not a bad mom, but that's not true. I served frozen pizza. I am in recovery for making a decision to drink instead of taking care of my children. I want to buy a motorcycle and drive off as far from my problems as I can. I am not all the positive things she wants me to say.

"Could you say that it's not the worst thing in the world to make frozen pizza? Or that you have had the courage to come in for help because you want to change instead of stubbornly continuing to drink and hurt your family?"

I can't argue with that even if I am a bad mom.

"I guess I could say that I'm not drinking today."

Jen smiles.

"That's the first positive thing you've said about yourself since you got here!"

Session 5

I'm on my way to Jen's. I park my car in front of the three story building. I grab my notebook and purse. I do my usual ritual of stopping in the bathroom before heading down the long hallway to Jen's office. I try not to look in the mirror, but it stretches across the entire wall and my reflection is hard to avoid as I wash my hands. I walk down the hall to the office door. The bell rings as I walk in. There's still no one else in the other therapists' offices, and I wonder how they afford the rent here. It's an older building, so maybe it's a lot cheaper than most places. It's definitely not like the therapist's office where we take Andy.

Andy's play therapist is part of a busy, new office complex. It's hard to find a parking place, which is frustrating because I'm always late. We enter the office on a marble floor and sign in with the secretary at a cherry, wood desk. We sit in the large waiting room where there are always several people waiting their turn. There are beautiful paintings on the wall and music pumped into the room through stylish speakers, but I like the atmosphere in Jen's office better. The carpet is old and the furniture is faded, but if we're in the middle of an issue we may go 15 or 20 minutes over my time. It's like I'm her only patient and she has all the time in the world for me.

I walk into Jen's office. She smiles at me as she looks up from the paperwork on her desk. I sit on the old, comfortable couch and sink in. She sits in her arm chair.

"How was your week?"

"It was okay."

"Just okay?"

I should have said I was fine. I hate answering these feeling questions. But I need to be honest. I'm agitated and don't know why. I need to think of some feeling words from the picture chart.

"I feel frustrated."

"What is making you feel frustrated?"

I want to run out of the room. I make myself come back mentally. My thoughts feel like they are on the Scrambler ride at the county fair. I can't slow them down long enough to see what's there.

"I don't know."

"Think of your week. What comes to mind?"

"I was really busy this week. It seems like I'm either bored or there's too much going on."

"Do you have a calendar?"

"At home I have one on the wall."

"Do you see it often?"

"Not often enough. I forget to look at it most of the time."

"So, how do you plan things or keep track of your schedule?"

"I don't. I just do what's in front of me at the moment. If I'm excited about something I don't forget. But if it's details and it's not in front of me, I forget about it."

"You need to get a pocket calendar that you can carry with you so you always have your schedule in front of you."

"Ok."

I get out my notebook and write that down. I wonder if I'll remember to look in my notebook this week.

"You are probably creating most of the chaos in your life yourself. A lot of people who grew up in chaotic homes become comfortable in that environment because it's what they know. Without realizing it, they create havoc in their lives because it's the only way they know how to function."

I cross my arms and look out the window. That's the most ridiculous thing I've ever heard.

"What is your schedule like?"

"It's all recovery stuff and my kids' activities."

"What was your life like before treatment and recovery?"

I smile a little. I don't even know where to start.

"I was homeschooling my kids, taking a class to finish my degree, writing skits for my church's Women's Ministry team, leading Bible studies, and running weekend retreats. I coached my kids' soccer and softball teams and was looking at how to add homeschool sports into the private school conference."

"And you took care of your home and meals too?"

"Oh, yeah, that too."

"That's a really full schedule."

"I like to keep busy."

"Why do you think you like to keep busy?"

"I don't like to waste time."

"Is relaxing a waste of time?"

"Yes. I mean people have to sleep, but I have thought it would be cool if I could learn to do that deep sleep thing so I would only need two-to-three hours of sleep a night. Then I could get so much more done."

"Have you ever thought that you keep yourself busy so you don't have to be alone with yourself and your thoughts and your feelings?"

I look out the window again. I am fascinated by Jen's question. I would never have thought of that, but it makes so much sense. She's right. I don't like being alone.

"I don't know. I never thought about it. I just don't feel good when I'm not getting things done."

"What kinds of things do you like to get done?"

"Well, there's always housework, but that doesn't really make me feel good. I guess I feel the best when I do something for my church, like write a skit or help out with our Bible study."

"Why does that make you feel good?"

"Because it makes me feel like I'm helping others, making them think differently, see God in a way they didn't see him before."

"How do you think God sees you?"

I'm quiet and still. I start thinking about the ways I've taught others about how much God loves them no matter what they've done or who they are. I've tried to write skits that move people in a way that they feel closer to God. But how does God see me?

"I think he sees me as someone he created for a purpose."

"For what purpose do you think he created you?"

"I think he gave me the talent to write and wants me to use it to help people."

Jen shifts in her chair and her eyes seem browner, almost black as she leans closer to me. She raises an eyebrow.

"Do you think God would think the same about you whether you were using your talent or not? If you didn't do another thing for your church do you think he'd still love you?"

I can't look away from her intense gaze. I feel like a rabbit caught in a trap. I know the answer is supposed to be yes, but I can't say that. I don't believe it. How can God think the same way about the person who's lying around on the couch watching soaps on TV and the person who sells their house to use the money to go to Africa to help millions of orphaned children?

"No, I don't think he would."

"So, you think you need to earn his love? Is that what you write about?"

"No! I write about his grace and love for people."

"So you're special then. The rules don't apply to you."

I move around on the couch. I'm hot and my heart is beating fast. She doesn't understand either. She is starting to sound like Nancy. Nancy keeps telling me life isn't about how much I do, but about who God says I am. No one understands me. I can't explain that inner drive to be the best at something. It's been there as long as I can remember. The drive to achieve something is like a train. It's so fast and powerful. There are no brakes. It never stops. It just goes and goes and goes.

"That's not what I mean."

"That's what you said."

"I know, but....I can't explain it."

"Listen, people can't keep themselves going 110 percent all the time without burning out. Alcoholics are often workaholics as well. And for the most part, people who are workaholics are just covering their fear of being alone and their fear of failure."

I'm letting her words roll around in my mind. I've been living at 110 percent for years. I don't know how else to do it.

"I would like to teach you some exercises to help you slow down your mind."

It sounds painful, but it might be a relief if I could get my thoughts to slow down enough to put them in order a little bit. Jen pushes a button on a little CD player that sits on her shelf by her teapot. Soothing music begins to play. I move around on the couch cushions trying to get comfortable.

"Close your eyes."

I close my eyes. The notes from the music float from the CD player to my mind.

"Take a deep breath in, and let it out slowly."

I listen to her breathe in and out. I take a deep breath in. As I breathe out, my shoulders roll inward and I put my hands between my knees. The weight of my thoughts pulls my head down.

71

"Take another deep breathe in and as you let it out, picture your anger and anxiety as the color red and you're pushing it out of your body as you exhale."

I try to visualize the color red inside my body. I have trouble seeing the color red inside me. The music continues to flow into my head and my brain is melting. I hear her saying something about breathing in a white light and breathing out the red. I'm trying to see the white light, but it's harder to see than the red. I take a deep breath and try to force the white light to appear. The music takes me to a beach with palm trees and white sand. I'm in Mexico with JB and we're walking along the beach listening to the waves crash against the shore and run up over our feet. It feels cold and tickles as it runs quickly and forcefully back to the sea. The shells disappear and reappear with every wave that washes in.

"Jenny."

I open my eyes. Jen is looking at me.

"Are you following?"

"I think I was with you for a while. I had a hard time focusing on the lights and I started thinking about the music and then I was in Mexico."

Jen pushes the button on CD player and the music stops.

"I don't think we're going to go any further until we get you tested for Attention Deficit Disorder (ADD)."

A wave of emotion washes over me as the tide of the Mexican daydream vanishes. Not going any further. I was just starting to feel comfortable talking. There's so much inside of me. I just want her to keep pulling things out of me until they stop torturing me. I've kept them buried for so long, and we're finally digging them out. But she stopped digging. And now she's taking our shovels and hanging them up. I feel mixed emotions, wanting to share my pain with someone, but relieved that I don't have to. On the other hand, ADD could be my answer. I've always wondered what was wrong with me. Why couldn't I concentrate in my classrooms growing up? Why did I always get caught staring out the window? Why couldn't I keep my house and life organized? ADD would make sense. Of course! This is the piece of the puzzle I've been missing for so long.

Jen changes gears and looks up a name for me: Dr. Randy Nelson. She hands me a piece of paper, and I copy down the clinic information.

"I want you to call him when you get home and make an appointment."

We talk about ADD for the rest of the session; what it is, how it works, why it makes life so difficult. I'm completely lost in this new development. Maybe this is the answer to all of my problems, and things will be so much easier once I get some ADD medication. I'm expecting a miracle as we end our session a little early, both of us invigorated by this piece of the puzzle. I can't wait to get home. I haven't been sharing much with JB about my sessions with Jen, and I don't like to talk to him about my feelings, but I can't wait to tell him ADD is the answer to all of our problems.

73

Session 6

I'm dragging a bag full of ADD books down the hallway to Jen's office. I bought them after leaving her office last week. I don't hesitate at the office door today because I'm excited to get inside and talk some more about this ADD solution. I've read a lot of chapters out of all four of the books and I've made my appointment with Dr. Nelson. I'm frustrated with JB's response. He doesn't believe I have ADD. Neither does Nancy. They think I'm just looking for a magic pill to make everything go away. So what if I am? From what I've read so far the magic pill works! I could have a normal life. I could have one long constant flow of thought without getting off track. ADD seems so obvious to me now. I don't know how they can't see it? What do they know? They think they know everything! I hate that! Jen is a therapist with a license. Plus, JB and Nancy are so logical. I know they don't understand me.

Jen hears me come in and barely has a chance to say anything before I walk up to her office door.

"Hi."

I walk in and sink into my spot on the couch. I have my books and calendar in a red bag I set on the floor.

"It looks like you brought some things with you today."

"Yeah, I bought a calendar, a wristband, some athletic tape and six books about ADD. I only brought four of them with me and I made an appointment with Dr. Nelson."

"Great! When is your appointment?"

"I couldn't get in until next week."

"That's great."

I pull the books out of my bag and set them on the couch.

"I've been reading a lot this week. My favorite book was, *Moms with ADD*. It explained what is expected in the role of being a mom vs. what the world actually gets with an ADD mom. It focused on the positive aspects of ADD like creativity and inspiration and a better ability to play with your kids. It also had a lot of great coping skills and information on medication."

I think I should feel as excited as I sound, but I feel empty. I feel like we hit a fork in the road and turned the wrong way. I can't wait to get to Dr. Nelson's office and get a confirmation of my ADD along with the magic pill that will change my life! But I'm worried that if I do have ADD, Jen will think that's the answer to my problems and she won't ask me anymore questions or try to draw out how I feel. What if this is one of the last times I get to sit on her couch? I breathe in deep and sit up straighter. I feel the few cracks we've made in the wall around my heart beginning to seal up.

Jen looks at the pile of stuff I brought.

"What is the wristband for?"

"Well, I bought the calendar and put my schedule in there, but it didn't help me remember what I needed from the grocery store or an errand, so I thought if I could write down everything I needed on my wrist every day, then I'd have it right in front of me where I couldn't forget it."

"That's a great idea! How did it work?"

"Well, it still needs some work."

My first trip with my wristband is out to the drug store where I not only need to pick up medications for JB, but I also need to get lunch bags and distilled water. I write all three things down on the athletic tape and wrap it around the wristband, which is on my arm. I pull my sleeve down over the wristband as I walk into the store. I walk down the card aisle and start thinking about my father-in-law because his birthday is coming up. I tell myself that I need to get him a card before the end of the month. I walk to the next aisle and stop. I don't know where I'm going. I think about what I need and remember the wristband. I look around to see if anyone is watching me. I don't see anyone. I pull up my sleeve and look at the list. Oh yeah, distilled water. I walk a few aisles down. Then I see the aisle with paper and pens, and I veer toward the pens. I love pens. I start looking at my favorites; the fine tip ball point pens. I grab a three-pack rationalizing to myself that it's ok to buy them since I've been doing so much journaling and recovery homework. It makes it easier to fill in the emotional blank spaces when I use my favorite pen.

I start walking down the aisle. Where next? I look at my wrist again. Oh yeah, distilled water. I need to focus. I walk down the next aisle and grab the distilled water. I look at my wrist again: lunch bags. This is kind of cool. I would have forgotten something by now, for sure! But I feel like an idiot. Who loses track of what they're looking for with each new aisle or item that attracts their attention?! I'm so stupid. I get the lunch bags and head toward the check out. I keep my eyes down on the counter so I don't have to meet the eyes of the cashier. I heave the gallon jug of water onto the counter and wince as I notice my wristband is sticking out. I look up at the cashier, but she doesn't seem to notice it. I slide my sleeve back down over the wristband. I pay, and she puts my receipt in the bag. She says to have a good day. I've already turned to walk away so I add a half-hearted, "You too." It's probably not very convincing. I climb into my van and sit behind the steering wheel. I can't help thinking about how stupid I am. I feel like I'm slower than the other people in the store. I wonder if I will ever feel like part of society again. I get home. That's when I realize I forgot to get the medications. It was even on my wrist!

"Has your calendar helped you keep track of your schedule?"

"When I remember to bring it with me."

"Your number one rule with your calendar should be that you don't schedule anything unless you have your calendar with you."

"That's a good idea."

I get out my notebook to write that down so I don't forget. I've found that I don't remember much of my therapy sessions unless I write it down.

"How did you do with your anger this week?"

I think back through the week. I can only remember bits of yesterday and the trip to the store.

"I was more depressed than angry this week."

"What made you feel depressed?"

"I feel that way most of the time when I don't feel angry."

"Do you know that anger is a form of depression?"

"No."

That's weird. Anger and depression seem completely opposite. Sometimes this therapy stuff doesn't make any sense.

"Many people with anger don't realize they are depressed, because it expresses itself in a different way."

It makes me think about one of my appointments with the psychiatrist at the treatment center. She wrote down that I have chronic depression. I asked what that meant. She said it meant I've had depression for many years. That sounded wrong because I was a very happy person until I started drinking. Now it makes more sense, because I've been angry for as long as I can remember.

"What do you think about when you're depressed?"

"Well…"

What do I think about? Mostly I don't think at all. I just exist. But it is better now than when the depression was at its worst. One day in particular stands out.

I'm sitting in my office. No one else is in the house. I've been sitting on this chair staring at the wall and I don't know how much time has passed. My head hurts. It's not like a headache. It's darkness. It's a black hole sucking the life out of me. It's not stagnant. It's active. It tortures me. I close my eyes and rock back and forth. It does nothing. It doesn't matter how I move, what I say, what I do. It follows me. It haunts me. I want to push on it to ease the pain like I do with a stomachache. I just want to ease the pain a little, but the pain is so deep, like a deep-tissue bruise that nothing can reach. Today is worse than usual. It stretches on like there is no beginning and no end. I just want it to go away. I start thinking of ways out. I think about getting into my car and letting the garage fill up with exhaust. I think about shooting myself. I think about a big bottle of pills. That's it. I think of a huge bottle and then lots of bottles. I pour handfuls into my mouth and swallow them down with a glass of water. I watch myself slowly fall asleep. I look so peaceful in my imagination. I drift away into Jesus' arms. He is holding me. There is no condemnation for those in Christ Jesus. I don't feel guilt, just relief. The thoughts of suicide relieve my mind just a tiny bit. It's all I can do. These thoughts draw me. I want to get closer to them. I go over this image again and again. My shoulders feel so heavy. Weights hold me to the chair. I feel like I can't move a muscle. I finally look away from the wall. I look at the clock. It seems like it's been an eternity. It's only been five minutes. I can't keep going. Someone has slowed the clock down to an impossible existence and I wonder why God is doing this to me. This must be what hell is like. No, I think it must be worse than hell. Nothing can compare to this deep, heavy darkness. It's like it will never end.

"It's not as bad as it used to be."

"Are you taking your medication?"

"Yes."

"How long have you been taking it?"

"I started it in the fall before I went to treatment."

"We should look into getting you something else if this isn't working."

"Ok."

"Something we touched on, but haven't really gone through is your diet and exercise. These are extremely important to your mental health. Are you still running every day?"

"I'm trying."

I know Jen thinks this is a good thing. And I think it's a good thing, but there is some huge tension with JB about my running. He always wants to know how long I'll be gone or where I'm going. I hate it! I can't stand that he wants to know where I am all the time. And Nancy has a totally different take on my running. She thinks I just switched one addiction for another. Well, at least with running I'm staying in shape. How bad can it be?!

"How are your eating habits?"

"Well, they're not great, but they're not bad."

"There's a great nutrition website I want you to go to. There are all kinds of books and other places to learn how to eat healthy. It's really important for your recovery, so I want you to keep track of your exercise and watch what you're eating. It's good to avoid caffeine, especially if you have ADD."

"Ok."

I'm all for the running, but I know before I even leave her office that I'm not going to look up a nutrition website. I'm also not giving up my Mountain Dew. I know there is caffeine-free Mountain Dew, but that seems like drinking non-alcoholic beer. What's the point?

Session 7

I'm in the bathroom of the office building staring at myself in the mirror. I wish I could figure out who I'm looking at. I wonder if I changed when I started drinking or maybe I never really knew myself in the first place. I walk down the long hallway to Jen's office. I go in. The doorbell rings. I walk back to her office.

"Come in."

I walk in and sit on the couch. I write the check and hand it to Jen. She is a little antsy like she has a lot of energy, and her eyes search mine as she asks about my ADD appointment.

"Did you have your appointment with Dr. Nelson?"

I get a folder out of my bag. I've taken so many tests and read so much information and heard so many different possible diagnoses that my head is spinning. I hand over a packet of information I got from Dr. Nelson's office. I don't know where to start.

"I guess I don't have ADD."

Jen looks surprised as she opens the packet.

"I took a lot of tests, like hours of tests over several days."

Jen scans the information.

"Dr. Nelson said I have a lot of other things, but I don't have ADD."

Jen begins to read bits of information.

"Eighteen of nineteen symptoms of Attention-Deficit/Hyperactivity Disorder are reported by Jenny: fidgeting or feeling restless; difficulty remaining satisfied; being easily distracted; losing important things or forgetting a lot; always feeling on the go, as if driven by a motor."

She moves on to the next area.

"On the *MMPI-2, Minnesota Multi-phasic Personality Inventory*, people with similar profiles are rebellious, feel inadequate, alienated, irritable, angry, argumentative, distrustful, and behave unpredictably. They see their world as threatening. They are often emotionally distant from others and unhappy. They present with a variety of social, sexual, and familial maladjustments. They have poor social judgment, are prone to act out, and impulsive."

I sit quietly listening, but my thoughts begin to drift elsewhere.

I'm sitting in a small white room with one window. The sun is shining in. I'm at the ADD clinic and a young man is getting another test ready. I've already taken some tests on the computer. Now this man is going to ask me questions. He's probably fifteen years younger than I am, but I feel like a kid in school again. I'm nervous because I want to do well on these tests. He asks if I'm ready, and I nod my head. He begins to ask me simple math questions. I answer them without trouble. Then he asks me a word problem. I start to sweat. I'm terrible at word problems. I could never do them in school. I have a pencil and paper to write down the numbers. I scribble a few notes down and give him an answer. I'm guessing it's wrong.

Next, he shows me the measure of a song with notes on the scale and I'm supposed to tell him the name of the song. I look at the notes: quarter note, dotted half note, two eighth notes. I start humming the notes to myself. I can hear the tune, but I can't think of the song. He waits patiently. I'm wracking my mind. Still nothing. I finally give up and say I don't know. We go on to the next question. As soon as I answer the next question the song title comes to mind and I blurt out, "America!" He looks at me funny. I tell him that's the name of the song. He smiles and writes it down. I can't believe I figured out the song. I feel so much better.

Jen begins to read more facts she finds of interest.

"Jenny scored in the 42nd percentile on the auditory test, but scored in the 96th percentile on the visual test indicating the possibility of auditory memory impairment."

I immediately think of our time with Dr. Nelson.

JB and I are sitting on a red leather couch waiting to hear the results from days of testing. Dr. Nelson turns to JB and asks him if he's had any issues with me listening to him. JB replies that it's been a problem throughout our whole relationship. I know it's been a problem because many of our arguments are over conversations I don't even remember having. I feel like he just makes stuff up. Then I wonder if I am really missing whole conversations, and I wonder if I'm really that stupid.

Dr. Nelson begins to explain how my brain works. It's not that I don't listen; I just don't take in much of what I hear. He said it's not like it goes in one ear and out the other. It never goes in, in the first place. He says my auditory processing doesn't allow me to hear or follow conversations in loud environments because my brain gives as much attention to the noises around me as it does to the voice I'm listening to. I also don't take in conversations where the voice is familiar or if there is an accent. So, basically, I only take in about 30 percent of what someone says.

JB starts crying. I don't know why this is so emotional to him until he explains that he's lived our whole life together thinking I don't care about him because I never listen to him. I had no idea how much this meant to him. Dr. Nelson gives us some tips on how to communicate better through active listening. I'm supposed to practice repeating what JB says and ask questions so I can focus better. Suddenly, so much of our fighting makes sense. No wonder he didn't think I loved him. No wonder I didn't remember a lot of our conversations. It's such a relief to get some answers.

Jen continues.

"Cognitive/learning tests indicate Jenny has average to high average intelligence."

Jen says she's not surprised, but in Dr. Nelson's office I feel as though someone picked me up off the streets and told me I'm royalty; the long lost daughter of a king. Maybe I can finish my college degree. If JB's moment of relief was finding that I wasn't ignoring him all these years, mine was finding out I wasn't stupid. It's the first time in my life that someone other than JB is telling me I'm smart. Most surprising is that my highest scores are in math and my lowest scores are in reading. I love to read and I hate math. I wonder if they mixed me up with someone else.

I think back on all my bad math experiences. One of my math teachers yelled at me every time I didn't finish my homework and made fun of me when I answered a question wrong. Another teacher became frustrated with me after I finally got up the nerve to ask a question. He proceeded to lecture the class on listening skills. Another one threw an eraser at my head when I'd fallen asleep in class. My worst memory was in 2nd grade.

We are studying the life of the pioneers. We eat corn bread, which I don't like. I don't think there's any sugar in it. Then we make costumes using construction paper for hats and shoe buckles. In keeping with the pioneer theme, at math time, our teacher asks us math questions. If we get it wrong we have to sit in the corner with the dunce cap on. I sink as low in my chair as I can so I won't be called on, but it doesn't work. She asks me to solve an addition problem. I try really hard, but my hands are sweaty, and I can't think. I answer, and I know it's wrong from the look on Ms. Kind's face. She tells me to go sit in the corner, and put on the dunce cap. I'm trying my hardest not to cry as I stand up and walk toward the corner. This is the longest walk I've ever taken. I take the cap and put it on my head. I climb onto the stool. Luckily I'm facing the corner because I can't keep the tears from rolling down my cheeks.

Jen flips through some more pages of the results before reading out loud again.

"Jenny has a low level of dopamine, further indicating the probability of ADD. Writings pertaining to reward deficiency deficit may well apply to Jenny's cognitive functioning. It is almost as if regular life does not provide enough excitement, or juice, for her to be satisfied. Therefore, she pursues activities which operate on this dopamine rich system in the brain."

This is the part I don't understand. The descriptions sound like ADD, but maybe I don't understand it as well as I think I do. If it's not ADD, then what? Does it mean there's not something I can take to become more organized like the people I've read about whose entire lives were turned around as a result of finding the right medication? I'm tired of analyzing everything. Between the excitement of realizing I'm not stupid and the confusion of having ADD symptoms without actually having ADD, I'm exhausted and my head hurts.

"Well, knowing you're a visual learner, we'll have to start doing more visual things like writing on the whiteboard or using the sand tray room instead of just talking."

"Ok."

Talking; I wonder if that means that we'll be getting back to sharing my feelings. Now my stomach hurts, too.

Session 8

We're driving to Jen's office. JB is with me this time. Jen asked me if I thought he would come. I knew he would. I'm nervous but a little excited at the same time. I haven't been able to tell JB how I feel, and I'm hoping Jen will be a good mediator for us. On the other hand I'm worried that I'll say something that will upset him, and we won't get it figured out in an hour, and I'll have to deal with him for a week without Jen's help.

We pull in, and I tell JB I have to use the bathroom. He waits outside for me. I keep thinking about the Harley Davidson dealership across the street. I start to dream about riding away on my motorcycle. It doesn't matter where I go. I just want out. Guilt eats away at me. I look in the bathroom mirror. I'm such a loser. I can't believe I was once happy and excited about life. I used to think I could help people. Here I am barely dragging myself out of bed in the morning.

I turn away from the mirror and force open the heavy bathroom door. We walk down the hall silently together. I open the door and we go inside. The surroundings are familiar to me, but it feels weird having JB in this private space. It's been a sanctuary, and I know I need to share myself with JB or we will never have a marriage, but I don't feel comfortable with him here. I realize my kids are the reason I'm willing to get out of bed in the morning.

They're also the reason I'm willing to sit in this office, scared and lonely, trying to share the inside of me with one other person in the world who might be able to help.

JB and I sit on the couch. I wish it was a little bigger. Jen sits in her chair. We do some small talk and Jen answers some of JB's questions about insurance and medical billing. I'm looking out the window into the parking lot. It's in pretty bad shape. The pavement is cracked and there are plenty of potholes. The paint dividing the parking spaces is almost completely gone. The landscaping is sparse, and the few bushes that remain are overgrown. The only reason the office building doesn't look abandoned is the handful of randomly parked cars and the regular smokers who gather around the main door for their break. Jen gets us started on the real reason we're here.

"Let's talk about communication today. Communication is one of the hardest things to do for married couples and one of the most important parts of marriage. So, I want you to think of something that happened recently that was a problem."

I usually try hard to forget our problems. I always go blank when I feel put on the spot. Fortunately, we just had a situation. I don't really want to bring it up, but it seems like the safest topic to talk about so I start first before JB comes up with something more difficult.

"I have one."

"Go ahead."

"A couple days ago JB came home and told me that the garage was a mess."

"And how did that make you feel?"

I think for a moment, remembering the feelings chart.

"I felt angry."

"Why were you angry?"

"Because I can't do everything."

Jen turns to JB. I breathe.

"JB, what did you mean when you said the garage was a mess?"

JB looks at Jen. He talks calmly. My hands are shaking. I tuck them under my legs.

"I was just making a comment. I wasn't saying I wanted her to clean the garage. I was just frustrated that it was so dirty, and I spoke my thoughts out loud."

Jen turns her head toward me.

"This is a very common problem among adult children of alcoholics. They have learned, as kids, to read between the lines. They were given mixed messages on a daily basis, so they have to depend on their interpretation of the situation for their emotional, and often times, physical well-being. They also have to remember to keep the secrets of the family and they are loaded with guilt. So family members from alcoholic homes never say what they mean, and they don't think anyone else does either. They don't take what you are saying at face value. They communicate by beating around the bush or they do a passive-aggressive type of manipulation where they might say they aren't upset but they will act as if they are. Then, they grow up and develop relationships with people outside of their family and wonder why they can't communicate."

Jen turns to me.

"JB is not saying he wants you to clean the garage. He is stating a fact. You are taking it personally because you are used to reading into what your parents were saying because they probably never said what they were really thinking."

I'm stunned. Did she just tell me I'm wrong? How can my feelings be wrong? We just learned about how our feelings aren't right or wrong. That can't be what she just said. She looks at me. I don't know what to say. I think she knows I'm lost.

"Did JB say that you should clean the garage?"

"Yes."

"What did you hear him say, and what are you thinking about when he makes the comment?"

"I feel like I'm getting yelled at."

"Why do you feel like you're getting yelled at?"

91

I feel her question digging inside of me for an answer. It feels like she is cutting into my heart and pulling out memories and feelings I didn't know were there. I don't know where they're coming from. Everything she is saying about alcoholic families hits so close to home. Normally my defenses go up by now because I feel threatened. It takes me back to age six.

My dad is home. I didn't hear him come in. I don't have time to hide in my room. Maybe I can sneak by. I jump off the couch and run toward the kitchen. He comes around the corner and I freeze. His voice is loud. He tells me to sit down. I turn around to sit at the table. Why didn't I go to bed earlier? He starts to talk about being tough in order to make it in this world.

"Come over here."

He's shouting. He doesn't think he is, but he always shouts when he's been drinking, like he's deaf. I stand up and walk around the table and stand in front of him.

"Life isn't easy. You gotta know how to defend yourself."

His voice is so loud I can't hear what he's saying. Mentally I'm trying to leave and listen to him at the same time.

"Hold your hands up like this."

He grabs my hands and holds them up in front of my face like I've seen on TV in boxing rings. Suddenly, he punches me in the side. I bend over. I'm shocked. Usually, he just talks for a long time when he comes home late, and all I have to do is try to stay awake. I stand up and clench my jaw. I tell myself not to cry. I need to be tough. He holds my hands back up and then he puts his hands up. I'm trying to be ready this time.

"Go ahead, punch your old man."

I'm not sure how to punch him or where, but I know I have to or I might get hit again. I swing toward his chest. He catches my hand in his and punches me with his other hand.

"See, you have to be quick."

I stay bent over for a few seconds. I don't think I can keep from crying this time. I don't know if the tears are from the pain in my stomach or the emotions I feel because he's hitting me. I can't let him see me cry. I breathe in deep and fight back the tears. I tell myself I'm tough and stop being a baby. I put my hands in the air again. I don't want to hit him because I know he'll hit me again after he blocks my punch, so I wait for him to make the first move. His hand moves toward my side so I grab it with both of my hands. He uses his other hand and slaps me across the face. It's not hard, but the emotional sting is killing me. He decides I've had enough. He pats my shoulder. He can tell I'm beginning to cry. I know I let him down. I'm not as tough as he was hoping I was. Letting him down hurts more than his punches. I tell him I'm going to bed. I run up the stairs and into my room. I jump underneath my covers and cry quietly into my pillow.

Jen asks me again how I feel. The pain is too close to the surface, and I can't answer the question without tears. I'm back in the room with JB, but I feel like I'm six again.

"I feel like nothing I do is good enough."

My voice cracks. Tears run down my cheeks. I take a deep breath.

"…like he's frustrated or mad at me all the time…like my dad used to be."

I look down. I can't see anything through the tears, and I can't stop them. I think of my dad. I think about how I could never do anything as perfectly as he wanted.

"So when you argue or JB makes a comment to you, you hear your dad?"

"I guess so."

It starts to make sense to me. I'm trying to pull it together and stop crying. I realize in that moment what I've known but haven't been able to overcome; our eight-year age difference and my feelings for JB interchange between being a safe father figure and being a husband.

"What we need to do is start using a communication tool so that you can both begin to understand what the other person is saying."

Jen grabs a communication work sheet and hands it to me.

"I want you to use this worksheet, and go through the situation."

I look at the worksheet. I wipe my cheeks with my sleeve. The work sheet says, "In this situation…"

"In this situation JB came home and told me the garage was a mess."

I look at the next part, "I felt…"

Feel. What did I feel?

"I felt angry."

I look down at the next line, "Because I need." Need! I don't need anything. I can't think. I stare at the floor. My thoughts are racing. I've never needed anything. I don't need anyone. I don't need anything. I can do it myself. I had to do it myself. Maybe I can skip this line. Jen notices my hesitation.

"Jenny, this is really important, but probably really hard, because you had to fend for yourself as a kid. Being self-sufficient was necessary when you were growing up, but now you are an adult, and you have to let go of those defense mechanisms in order to relate to other people. When thinking about needs, try to think about what you want."

What I want? I get to ask for something I want? That sounds so foreign, but it feels kind of good to think about what I want. It also scares me. When I wanted something as a kid, I was always disappointed, so wanting something was risky. It was so much easier to not expect anything than to be disappointed.

"We all have needs that have to be met. You may have suppressed your needs, but you still have them. What do you want from JB in this situation?"

95

"I want him to help me clean the garage."

"So, you need help."

"Yeah."

"Good. Read the next part on the work sheet."

"Would you be willing to…"

"This is the request. You have a need and you are going to ask JB to meet the need by doing something."

"Would you be willing to help me clean the garage?"

"Now say the whole thing straight through."

"When you came home and complained about the garage being a mess, I felt angry because I need help. Would you be willing to help me clean the garage?"

I feel weird. I feel naked and vulnerable, but good. My body relaxes a little and I'm not as angry. I feel…softer. It's the first time I've asked JB for help with anything. It might be the first time I've asked anyone for help with anything.

Session 9

I'm on my way to see Jen. JB isn't with me today. I can't do two of those communication sessions in a row. I need a break. I want my time with Jen all to myself. She looks me in the eye, and her words are warm and comforting. Even if she is trying to be tough with me on a subject, it makes me love her more for it. She is the closest thing I've come to having a mom besides Nancy. I would never say that out loud. It seems too weird or unacceptable to talk about a friend like that, but Nancy isn't like any of my other friends. Being my Bible study leader, she was a mentor before we became friends. There doesn't seem to be a lot of difference to me between a parent and a mentor, but maybe that's because I'm not really sure what a parent is supposed to do. Nancy is not a people pleaser. She's direct, but kind. She gives me advice based on wanting what's best for me versus what I want to hear. My stubborn, independent streak normally makes me run from people like her, but she is different from the other people in my life who think they know what's best. Nancy loves me just the way I am. Love scares me, but I so desperately want it. It keeps me from running away.

I feel like I'm crossing a boundary when I think about Jen and Nancy filling the void my mom couldn't fill. When I think of my own mom, it's a blur. My mom had so many things going on at once; seven kids, an alcoholic husband, a trashed house and her church work. As a Mormon trying to earn her way into heaven, her work was never done. She was always running a hundred miles an hour. Maybe that's where I get it.

The hardest part about being mad at my mom is that she tried so hard. If she had said mean words or abused me somehow, I would feel justified in my anger, but she was nice. She made Halloween costumes and baked cookies for school. She came to my sports games and cheered me on. She drove me to countless soccer games and somehow found money for me to play on summer teams. She never raised her voice. So, how could I resent her so much?

I explained my mom to a psychiatrist once who said she probably has obsessive-compulsive disorder. I'll probably never really know. I just wanted her to notice me. Even though she was there physically a lot of the time, it was like she wasn't there. Her body was with us, but her mind was somewhere else. Her two favorite movies were *Somewhere in Time* and *The Two Worlds of Jennie Logan,* where the main characters go back in time to be with the person they love. I think my mom lives in another time always trying to get back to her mom. I don't think she'll ever know how much she is missing in the present by living in the past. When I think of my childhood without healthy parents, I get sad, lonely, and often very angry, but when I think of the repercussions on my siblings, it infuriates me.

I'm home from college. I'm not living at home, because there isn't any space, but I come back to visit and check up on my little brothers and sisters. Like usual there are kids everywhere and not everyone is accounted for. We usually find Jeff out in the woods somewhere with a box of matches and a big knife. Ben and Sam are in the garage with a dummy they made from old clothes and newspaper and whatever else they found lying around. They have a video camera they're using to tape something for school. I'm really impressed that they are actually doing some schoolwork and that's when they light the dummy on fire.

I walk into the house and step over backpacks, shoes, and boxes of stuff. Jessica is sitting at the table doing her homework. As I get closer I see she is crying. She sees me right away and wipes the tears away as she runs over to give me a hug. I squeeze her tight and ask her what's wrong. She breaks down again, only now she is crying so hard I can't understand what she's saying. I finally get it out of her that she is having a hard time with her math homework. I sit down with her to look at it, and I'm shocked to see the level of difficulty for fifth grade. I start looking through her math book to see the examples so I can help. That's when she starts crying harder. She tells me she is in the dumb class, and everyone else is smarter than she is. I ask her why she thinks she's in the dumb class, and she tells me that she has to leave school on the little bus and go on field trips with her small group of dumb kids who can't keep up with everyone else.

My heart breaks. I know exactly what she's talking about because I went to the same school at her age. She's in the Omnibus program. Only the top five percent of the whole grade gets to participate in the program. They get out of school for special field trips, and they are in high level classes. Everyone knew who the smart kids were, and I was jealous every time they got to leave class to go on their special trips. It's almost the end of the school year, and it hits me that not only did she miss out on a self-esteem boosting experience, but my poor little sister has believed all year that she is stupid! I explain to her several times what the program really is and that she's actually one of the smartest kids in her class, but she doesn't believe me. She thinks I'm just trying to make her feel better. No matter how many different ways I try, she doesn't go for it. I suppose after an entire year of thinking she's dumb, one little conversation with her sister who is home from college isn't going to sway her.

I'm so mad at my parents I could burn their house down, but that isn't going to help Jessica. I'm mad at myself for not being home to have caught this earlier. It makes me question if going to college was the right thing to do. It seems so impossible to pick up all the pieces left behind by my mom and dad, but I love my siblings too much to give up.

I'm almost to Jen's office. I feel anxious, but excited at the same time. I love my hour with Jen, but I hate that it's only once a week. I get anxious that the hour I have won't be spent well, and that I'll have to wait a whole week to see her again. I'm hoping that we talk about my feelings because I feel more connected to her, but it also makes me sick to my stomach. I feel like I'm beginning to let down my guard with her. I think that would make life feel less heavy.

I walk down the long hall trying to avoid people like usual. The hall doesn't seem as long as it did the first few weeks, but it's still a little nerve wracking. I reach for the doorknob and turn it. It doesn't turn. My heart drops. I turn it again. It's locked. My heart races. I don't want to turn around. I don't want anyone to see me. I couldn't be more embarrassed if I was naked right here in the hallway. I don't know what to do. I think quickly. I look at my watch. I'm not early. I open my purse and pull out my calendar. I have it written down. We usually meet at 1 p.m., but we changed this time to 10 a.m. I bet she forgot.

The weight on my shoulders makes it hard to move. I push myself to walk back down the hall. I see a man walking into the building. I look at the floor. He holds the door open for me. I mumble, "Thanks." I get in my car and sit. Inside I'm fighting with myself. Part of me is rebuilding the wall around my heart. Another part of me is trying to stop. I want to break it down. The loneliness is killing me! I'm racing through ideas and excuses, trying to find an explanation or an answer that will satisfy my heart, but nothing is working. My drive home aches. A fight breaks out. My mind is bombarding me with old messages of worthlessness. My dad's voice is shouting that I should never have gone to therapy in the first place. I don't need counseling. I don't need anyone. I can do it myself. The lonely little girl inside me is begging me not to rebuild the wall. She is desperate for love and for someone to know her. She keeps glimpsing small slivers of hope, but feels every time she grasps one, she gets cut. I need a drink. This battle is exhausting. I don't want to fight it anymore. I just want out.

Session 10

It was hard to go two weeks without my therapy session. I get anxious at the end of one week. Two weeks was really hard. I'm mad at her for not being there last week, but my anxiety is so high that I don't care what she did as long as she is here today. I pull into the parking lot.

I walk down the long hall and stand in front of the door. I'm afraid to turn the doorknob. What if it's locked again? I can't handle that twice. I'm trying to pretend that I didn't feel rejected last week, but it's not working. If I pretend I didn't feel rejected, I have to pretend that I don't care. I do care. I just don't want to admit it.

I stand in front of the door. I look down the hall to see if anyone is watching. I can't do this with someone watching. No one is in the hall. I take a deep breath and turn the knob. It opens. I exhale, letting out two weeks' worth of anxiety. I walk in and stand still for a minute. Her office door is open, but I don't want to go in. I don't know what to say. I can't confront people.

"Come in."

I walk to the office. I try to look fine. I sit in my spot on the couch. She looks at me and smiles. The warmth of her smile melts my resolve. I tell myself that everyone makes mistakes. And Jen, although a professional, is a little scattered and unorganized like me. I understand. I just don't want it to happen again.

"How did you do for two weeks?"

"Fine."

It was not fine! I need to tell her the truth, or I'll never get better.

"Actually, it was kind of hard."

"I'm sorry I wasn't here, but I'm glad you got a chance to see that you can make it two weeks if you need to."

"Yeah."

I want to ask her how long she'll let me come here. Missing a week scared me and made me aware that I can't keep coming forever.

"Is there a certain number of sessions that I get before I'm supposed to be done?"

Jen changes modes. She sits up and looks me in the eye.

"There are a lot of therapists who believe that you should only be with a client for six-to-eight weeks."

I squirm in my chair because it's been more than eight weeks and I don't even feel like I've gotten started yet.

"Another group of therapists think there's a need to go back to a person's childhood to find the root causes of their beliefs and behaviors. That can last as many weeks or months as it takes. I work closer to that belief, but I also think each client is different. I really try to take each person as they come and let the Holy Spirit guide us."

I knew she was a Christian counselor, but I didn't know how much she relied on God in our sessions. Some of our sessions make more sense now, the way we shift gears suddenly from one thing to another and hit on something important. She seems to be able to find the things we need to talk about without a very systematic approach. Knowing she is letting God guide her makes me feel slightly more secure. My desire for security reminds me to ask her about DBT, a therapy I'd heard about during the week.

"Have you heard of DBT?"

"Yes, why?"

"I saw that psychiatrist you wanted me to see about my medications. We had a very nice talk, and she mentioned that DBT might be good for me. Then, I was with Andy's therapist for a parent meeting, and she said the same thing. I can't remember what the letters stand for. Do you know what I'm talking about?"

"Dialectical Behavior Therapy. It was designed for people with Borderline Personality Disorder, but it teaches skills that anyone can benefit from."

She pauses. I get the feeling she doesn't think I need it. I begin to wonder if I have Borderline Personality Disorder. I'll look it up when I get home.

"It just seemed weird that I'd never heard of it before and then two different therapists tell me in one week that I should look into it. Andy's therapist even gave me some places where they have DBT programs."

"Well, my church started a DBT group. They are in the experimental phase so they are just taking people from our church, but I will talk to Terri. She is the person heading it up. Maybe we can get you into a group there."

"Ok."

I feel relieved. I feel like I'm supposed to go, like God is steering me that way, but I don't know how to say that. I'm glad she's going along with me on this.

"The DBT program requires a long commitment; six-to-twelve months."

Every nerve in my body melts. Six-to-twelve months is security. It means I won't have to worry each week whether this might be my last. The more I open up, the greater my fear grows that it won't last long, like it's too good to be true.

"I was recently trained in Dialectical Behavior Therapy. Since it was developed for people with Borderline Personality the group contains people with a lot of issues and behavior problems. I just don't want you to be shocked when you get there."

Shocked. I don't think anything could shock me like my first day in treatment.

It's Friday afternoon. JB is driving. We are heading out of the security of our suburban Woodbury home to the city where I'm supposed to go for chemical dependency treatment. The drive is long and quiet. I have a bag with a few days' worth of clothes, my journal and some toiletries. We enter through a back door off the parking ramp. The hallway is empty. We ride an elevator to the third floor. Two large wooden doors guard the entrance to the Mental Illness/Chemical Dependency wing. JB opens the door. I take a deep breath. The noise level jumps immediately. People are coming and going. There's an older man in a ripped shirt with scraggly hair sitting in a chair in front of us getting his blood pressure checked. Another woman is standing at the counter asking for her meds. The look in her eyes is desperate, but the nurse doesn't look up from her work as she tells the woman it's not time yet. Another nurse walks by me in a hurry. A big lady at the counter asks for my name. She looks at a board on the wall next to her. She asks who is with me. I tell her that he is my husband. She says that he can leave now. I panic. I thought he could help me to the room, maybe stay for a little while. A man walks up to JB to escort him out the door. I grab his arm in desperation. I turn to the nurse and ask her if she knows how long I'll be here. A nurse behind me laughs and says I could be here for 30 days. My mind races and the room feels like it's spinning. The man is showing JB out the door. Tears stream down my face. I want to run into his arms and go home. He kisses me goodbye. He's crying too.

The big lady at the desk asks for my bag. I look at her. Her request doesn't register right away. I'm still panicked that I'm alone now in this scary place. I put the overnight bag on the counter. I'm still thinking about running out the door. There has to be another way. My head is still spinning. The nurse opens my bag and starts looking through it. I feel violated, and I'm beginning to realize I'm not capable of walking away from here. I don't have the mental capacity to reason or make a decision. My desire for alcohol has taken over, and I'm not just a prisoner at this hospital; I'm a prisoner in my own body. She pulls out my travel-size mouthwash and throws it in the garbage. Then she pulls out my depression medication and puts it on the counter. She puts everything else back into the bag and hands it to me. I can't believe I brought the mouthwash. Now they think I was trying to bring alcohol into treatment. I think about telling her that I had no intention of drinking it, but I realize they won't believe me. I'm scared I won't get my medication. I need it. What if I spiral down into that huge dark pit again? I'm not sure I can make it out again.

Another nurse has me sit down in the chair where the old man was. She puts the blood pressure cuff on me. The nurse looks at the cuff a little funny and says my pressure is normal. She writes it down and asks me my height and weight. I'm thinner than I should be. My cheeks are sunken and I have more lines on my face than a 34 year-old should have. She puts a thermometer in my mouth. A woman walks in the big wooden door. She stares at me like I stared at the last guy in the chair. The nurse takes out the thermometer, writes something down and tells me I'm in room 10. I look down the hallway. I look back at her. I don't know what to do. She points and says it's straight down the hall. I start walking. There are people in the hallway. I look at the floor. Every step takes me further from my comfort zone and into the unknown. Three young men lean against a wall talking. They have on baggy jeans, headbands and muscle t-shirts. An older woman with oxygen tubes in her nose sits in a wheel chair.

She's being pushed down the hall by a thin woman with scraggly dark hair. Another girl is talking on one of the pay phones. She's in sweatpants, and her hands shake as she yells into the phone and then starts crying. I hate this place.

I look at Jen. Borderline Personality Disorders don't sound very scary after being in a treatment facility that specializes in mental illness.

"Since I had depression while in treatment, I was put in the mental illness outpatient group with schizophrenic and bipolar alcoholics. I think I'll be ok."

"I'll talk to Terri. She will probably need to meet with you beforehand to see if you meet the requirements. "

I hope this works out. Even though my stomach turns over when I think about opening up to people, I sense that the constant loneliness and depression I feel could go away if I could keep trying to share myself with people. I just need to keep working at getting off the island I live on.

"Okay."

I wonder what kind of requirements I have to meet. Maybe I have to be mentally ill enough to be there. I don't think I am. But maybe I'm sicker than I think I am. Sometimes I feel like I'm healthier than the people in my twelve step group, and other times I feel like I have more issues than all the other members put together. Jen moves onto a new topic.

"Let's talk about hobbies. What do you enjoy doing in your spare time?"

I hate this question. I've heard it a half dozen times, mostly in my Bible studies as a conversation starter. Everyone has lovely answers like shopping, going to the spa, getting their nails done, reading a book. I can never think of anything so I just repeat what someone else says. I decide to be honest with Jen.

"I don't know. I never have spare time."

"Something adult children of alcoholics do is to try to make every moment of everyday a productive one. They don't know how to relax, and they don't know that it's okay and healthy to have some down time."

I don't know what she's talking about or how to relate this to my life. There are too many things that need to get done in a day. If I want to catch up with all of those, I can't just sit around and read a book. I allow myself to read self-help books, because it improves my production. The only novels I read are required reading for classes.

"Is there anything you and JB like to do together?"

"We go to movies sometimes. Once we went golfing, but that didn't go so well."

"What do you mean?"

I try to come up with words to describe how JB and I interact. We're like fire and water. I'm the fire that burns slowly, exploding unexpectedly at times. JB is the calm

109

water attracted to the danger of the flames, and prone to put them out.

We are standing on the range at the golf course. I place my hands on the grip like JB showed me. It feels funny with my fingers intertwined. I pull the club back over my shoulder. It feels like a baseball swing, so I know I'm doing something wrong. JB tells me to keep my elbow straighter. I straighten it out and feel more awkward than ever. It's making me feel anxious. I swing and the ball dribbles off the tee and rolls five feet in front of me. I grab another ball out of the wire basket and place it carefully on the tee. JB says I need to keep my eye on the ball. I line up my feet. JB says my feet should be further back from the ball. I think JB should stop talking now. I pull the club back again and check my elbow. I focus on the ball, hold my breath and swing. I hit the top of the ball and it rolls out just another foot farther than my first one. JB says I shouldn't hold my breath. I want to hit JB with my club. I grab another ball, line up my feet, and bring my club back. This time I completely miss the ball. I want to scream and throw my club across the range. JB doesn't say anything. He knows I'm close to my breaking point. There's nothing he can say to help me because I am all emotion now, and I can't hear anything. I only feel hot, red anger boiling inside me.

JB turns to his own bucket of balls. His first shot goes at least 200 yards. He reaches for another ball. He's ignoring me now. I put another ball on the tee. I take a few deep breaths and try to let go of the tension. I try to tell myself that this is supposed to be fun, but it doesn't work. It never works. I go through half of my bucket of balls with little improvement. I watch JB swing again. He has so much power behind his swing. The harder I swing the more I miss the ball. I ask him for some more help. He turns slowly. I try to sound calm and defeated so he'll help me. As much as I don't like asking for help, I can't give up, because something inside me says I will keep swinging until I hit a decent ball. He might not believe that my anger is under control, but he is willing to help me again. He gives me a few more tips about how I'm holding the club and how to shift my weight. I'm starting to feel the difference between my baseball swing and a golf swing. I finally connect with the ball and it feels right and the ball sails to the second flag. JB says I hit it 75 yards. I should feel happy, and I do feel better, but I'm disappointed it took me so long. I put on a fake smile. I don't know why I fake one because he knows the difference.

"I'm pretty competitive, and I get angry when I can't do something well. It took me awhile to hit the ball, so it wasn't very fun for either of us because I was angry most of the time."

Maybe I'm not as laid back as I think I am. My whole life I've claimed to be a laid back, go-with-the-flow kind of person. Nancy has contended that I'm more controlling than I think. I didn't believe her until now. Maybe I've just been telling myself I'm laid back because I feel so out of control, and I can't handle it. I think JB has been trying to say this for years, but he gave up. Nancy never gives up but she doesn't have to live with me. I wonder how long water can exist with fire.

"Let's make a list. You have homework for this week. I want you to come up with ten things that you can do for fun; things you enjoy."

111

"Ok, I'll try."

I pack up my things and head out of the office. This could easily take the whole week. I get into my car and sit. I like to just sit and think over our sessions before I drive home while the information is still fresh on my mind. Even more so I don't like to leave Jen's office. She makes me feel good. I get out a piece of paper and write the numbers one through ten on the side of the sheet. I stare blankly out the window. I see the Harley Davidson billboard. Yes! I've thought of something I like to do just for fun. There's no rhyme or reason for riding a motorcycle except they save on gas. I've always pictured a romantic escape from my life, riding my bike into the sunset. But even if I had nowhere to go and no reason to go, I love riding. I write it down on my list. Only nine more to go.

Session 11

I made my list of ten fun things to do with my spare time. About five of them are lame and I added them just to fill up the page. I really like the first two, but I feel guilty at the same time. It doesn't seem right to waste my time doing something unproductive. It's hard to imagine doing something for myself that's completely unproductive.

I pull into the parking lot, grab my list and head into Jen's office. Her office door is open so I stand in the doorway. She's sitting at her desk writing something. She has her glasses on and she looks unusually organized. Her smile warms me all over like it does every week. I go sit on the couch and write out my check.

"How was your week?"

Her voice is filled with life. It picks me up out of the seat cushions, like a hot air balloon.

I start with the appointment I had with Terri about the Dialectical Behavior Therapy group.

"I saw Terri this week about the DBT group."

"Really, that was quick."

"Yeah, I called and was able to meet with her on Wednesday. I filled out the forms, and she said I could jump in because they just started the second session."

I'm in Terri's office. Her desk sits next to two other desks in a small, somewhat defined space. Her desk is filled with papers. A picture of her family is tucked next to her desk lamp. A few comic strips are tacked to the grey wall dividers along with some inspirational posters. I sit on a chair next to her desk. I'm in the walkway of the other two desks. Even though no one else is at their desk and we seem to be in this office space alone, I have little sense of privacy. It doesn't matter though because I'm desperate to get into her group. She starts asking me some simple questions about me and my family. Then she gets to some of the harder questions.

"Have you ever felt suicidal?"

I think about my worst days of depression and carefully choose words to describe the depth of my feelings without giving her the idea that I might still feel that way.

"Yes."

"Have you tried to commit suicide?"

"No. I only thought about it."

"Did you ever have a plan?"

"I never had a real plan. I only had ideas about how I'd like to do it. I didn't go through with anything."

"Are there any other factors that are leading you to participate in this group?"

"I'm a recovering alcoholic."

"Did you get help for your alcoholism, and how long have you been in recovery?"

"I went to treatment in January, so it's been about three months."

She asks me some more questions, but they seem more methodical than informational, and I think she is satisfied that I have enough issues to be part of the group. I don't know if that's a good thing, but I'm happy I passed.

I reach into my bag and hand Jen a contract I signed in order to be in the DBT group. The contract is about making a commitment to the group. I suppose most of us with mental illness or addictions are not the most reliable or dependable people. But this contract means something more to me. The contract says that I am committed to attending group every week for one year, and I am not allowed to be in the group without doing one-on-one therapy in conjunction with the group. This means I have to see Jen for a whole year. If Jen signs this I don't have to worry every week about whether or not this will be the last session. It's impossibly hard to fight myself every week to share something when I'm constantly afraid of being rejected. Maybe if she signs this it will be easier to tell her what's in my head and how I really feel.

"This is the contract we have to sign."

Jen takes the contract. My hand is shaking. I tell myself I drank too much coffee this morning, but I know it's really fear and anxiety. If she doesn't agree to this I don't know what I'll do. I feel my heart preparing to shut down just in case she doesn't think this is a good idea. I'm trying not to let myself be hopeful, but it's too late. I let Jen get her foot in the door of my emotions weeks ago, and now I can't close it. She puts on her glasses and skims through the contract. I don't think she has any idea how much this means to me. If she doesn't sign this I might as well quit coming, because it'll just be a waste of money.

Jen takes off her glasses and puts the piece of paper on her lap.

"You know this is a big commitment, right?"

"Yes."

"You'll have to fill out diary cards and be there every week as well as coming here."

"I know."

She looks down at the contract again. I can tell by her tone of voice she thinks this is overkill, which makes me think I've masked my feelings again, as usual, and have appeared to be much healthier than I really am. I realize that I'm holding my breath, and I try to let it out slowly so she doesn't hear it. She reaches for her pen and signs her name at the bottom next to mine, then hands it back to me.

"Here you go."

I try to hide my relief, but I'm sure it's obvious as I take a deep breath and let my shoulders relax into the cushions of the couch. As my fear of rejection subsides, the fear of actually digging up my emotions starts to swell. I tuck the contract carefully into my bag. Jen stands up and grabs one of the dry erase markers.

"Today we're going to do a storyboard."

Jen draws a line across the white board.

"We're going to draw out your life in a storyboard format, highlighting your most memorable experiences. I want you to think about your earliest memories. Not just the good or bad ones, but anything that really sticks out."

Memories flash through my mind. Some of them are surprisingly pleasant. Some are not.

"What's the earliest memory you can think of?"

I race back through pictures of myself at all different ages and I see the earliest one I can think of.

"I think the earliest thing I remember is my fourth birthday. It was the night before my party, and my mom had made a train cake. I was sitting by the heater vent trying to tie my shoe."

I pause for a moment as I travel back to being four. In our old farm house the heater vents are big and square and when the heat comes on I curl up in front of them like a kitten and let the heat blow up my nightgown.

117

"I was determined to learn to tie my shoe. I remember finally getting it and being really proud of myself. I also remember being excited for my birthday the next day."

Jen writes on the board, "4th birthday; tied shoes."

"Good, can you think of some more things that stand out?"

I think of the lake I grew up on, one of my favorite places to go and get away from the world.

I'm walking down the long dirt road on the way home from school. Instead of heading up the driveway to my house, I keep walking. I go down the carpeted trail to the lake. I shuffle down the steep slope to the dock. Underneath some leaves between the birch trees I find the fishing poles. In a small clearing a shovel sticks up out of the dirt. I dig up some worms and put them in the ice cream bucket that is hanging from a nail on a tree. I sit on the end of the dock and put the worm on my hook. I throw the line out and watch the bobber hit the water. It bounces around until it sits still on the surface. I can see little sunfish gathering around the hook taking turns nibbling at my worm.

Lots of pictures begin to float through my head of when I was younger; my friend and I sneaking into the neighbor's detached garage and sitting behind the oversized steering wheel of her Model T car, rowing our boat across the lake to an abandoned house where we run up the staircase that is attached to the only remaining wall, walking along the old wooden timbers of the trolley car tracks pretending to be gangsters from the 1920s searching for our hidden loot.

In between all these fun memories, one bad one keeps intruding into my thoughts, and I can't get it out of my mind.

I'm six years old, staring out the window of my school bus. I feel a tug on my hat. It's winter, and I'm wearing my favorite hat. It's blue and white with penguins on it and a black and white pom-pom on top. Some older boys are sitting behind me. I feel another tug on my hat. The boys start laughing. I don't want to turn around. I'm scared. No one else is sitting by us. I feel my hat pull again. I look out the window. We're close to my stop. The boys keep pulling my hat. They are laughing really hard now. I stare out the window trying to think of something else so I don't cry. Something falls onto the seat next to me. It's a few black and white pieces of yarn. I realize they are pulling out the strings to my pom-pom. I can't keep the tears from coming. They stream down my face. I wipe a few of them away with my mitten trying not to look obvious. My stop is coming, and I don't dare move until we're there. The bus stops. I get up without turning around. I pick up my backpack and get in line with the neighbors. I try to wipe away the rest of my tears so no one sees them.

The older kids at my stop live in the opposite direction, and I quickly walk away. I walk until I think I'm far enough down the road that no one is watching. I take off my hat. There's nothing left of the pom-pom. They pulled out all the yarn. I can't hold back the tears anymore, and I start crying. My hat looks weird without the pom-pom. It would have been easier if they had just hit me. I think about home. My mom is probably busy. She won't notice me, but I can't be crying when I get home. I try to stop, but it's hard. I feel like a baby. I can't be a baby. I feel

119

pathetic. I can't let people hurt me. I have to be strong. I promise myself I'll never cry again. I dry my tears, crease my eyebrows, and set my jaw tight. I shove my hat deep inside my backpack so I don't have to explain the missing pom-pom to my mom in case she sees it.

"There was this time when I was six and I was coming home from school. Some bigger boys on the bus pulled out all the yarn to the pom-pom of my favorite hat. On my way home I made up my mind that I would never cry again."

Jen shifts in her chair and leans forward.

"You remember thinking that you would never cry again."

"Yeah, I remember that day really well."

"Why did you decide not to cry anymore?"

"I knew I had to be tough. I didn't have anyone to go to."

"Did you tell your parents?"

"No. I never told them anything."

"Why not?"

My dad was never home and if he was he'd tell me to stick up for myself. My mom might have been home, but she wasn't really available to talk to."

"So, she wasn't emotionally available?"

"That's a good way to put it."

"So, you were on your own at six?"

"I guess so."

"That is so sad."

Jen's eyes get red and her voice cracks. Her sympathy reaches me, and I feel the crust around my heart melting. Jen writes down, "Never cry again – age 6."

"How about some preteen or teen memories."

I start to think about being a teenager. I picture my school, my friends, my neighborhoods. As I think of my neighborhood friends, my shoulders feel heavy. My eyes move from the windows to the ceiling to the floor. I have a hard time moving. I feel frozen. My mind isn't racing anymore, it's just blank. There's no more color in my memories, just black and white images that scroll slowly across the screen in my mind. I have to concentrate to see the details of the scenes. I want to get up and walk out. I think about the Harley Dealership and getting that motorcycle. I remind myself I have to get better. I need to stay in this room mentally and focus. I force myself to look at the scenes in my mind that are scrolling by. Images from several memories pop in and out. One memory stops scrolling. It just sits in front of me. I try to make it scroll away so I can see something else, but it doesn't move. I don't know how to talk about this memory, so I back up a bit before starting.

"I started drinking pretty early."

Jen nods her head slowly. She sets down the marker and listens attentively, never taking her warm brown eyes off of me.

"One of my friends was a neighbor. She had an older brother and two older sisters who had a lot of parties. Usually we weren't welcome, but one night they didn't bother to kick us out."

The memory is sketchy. It was so long ago, and I was so drunk I don't remember everything. I try to put the pieces together.

"I liked this one boy."

Jen's voice is soothing and calm.

"How old were you?"

"Fourteen."

She waits for me to continue.

"I had a lot to drink. It was one of the first times I drank other than the beer my dad gave me. I remember sitting on the couch because I couldn't stand up anymore. I remember the feeling of being drunk was kind of scary, but felt really good."

I pause. I don't want to talk about it anymore. I'm trying to think of something else. I need to change the subject. I try to talk about anything else, but I can't get the images out of my head.

"I don't remember how, but I remember being in a bedroom with this guy."

My body tingles. I look at the floor. I cross my arms and legs. Somehow, just thinking about it makes me feel like it's happening again, and I want to curl up in a ball and stop talking. I look down into my lap.

Jen is quiet. The air in the room is heavy.

I can't look up at Jen. I can't talk. I'm trying, but I can't say anything. She's waiting. I hate the silence.

"I made a really bad mistake."

"Can you tell me about it?"

I take a deep breath and let it out slowly.

"I don't remember if he did it or I did, but one of us took my clothes off."

I'm looking down at my shirt. The buttons are being undone.

"The next thing I remember was being in bed with him."

I can't sit still anymore. I feel sick. I'm cold. Goose bumps cover my arms. I move around on the couch some more. My eyes dart around Jen's office. I'm looking at things but I don't really see them. She says nothing. I want to move on, go to the next thing. I'm done talking. I look out the window at the parking lot. It doesn't matter where I look, I can't stop the images flashing through my mind.

123

He is on top of me. My head sinks into the pillow so far I feel like I'm drowning. He pushes himself inside of me, and the pain wakes me from the dreamy state the alcohol has put me in. Tears stream down the corners of my eyes.

I can't think anymore and I push the fast forward on my memory to speed past the event.

"I don't know if I passed out or fell asleep, but I remember waking up in the morning. I found my clothes, put them on, hurried out of the house and walked my bike home."

My senses have come alive, and I'm surprised by how much detail I remember.

I hear the crunch of the rocks under my bike tires. I'm praying no one is watching me. I tried to get on my bike, but sitting on the seat was excruciating, so I'm walking it. I want to run, but it hurts too bad to walk any faster. I don't know where to go. I can't go home like this. I decide to walk my bike down the trail that goes through the woods. I have to go home sometime. But will anyone notice I'm not the same person that left the house yesterday? Probably not, but I need to wait until I can think. I need to figure out what to do. I would do anything to turn back time and wake up in my own bed.

Hours later after finding the courage to walk home, I stand in front of the mirror in my bathroom. It's been less than 24 hours since I left my house, but it might as well be years, because the tarnished girl I see now is barely recognizable compared to the young, innocent girl I saw yesterday.

I finally look up. My eyes travel from my lap to the floor to Jen's shoes to the chair to Jen's clipboard resting on her lap. I can't look any higher than that.

"So, at fourteen years old you were raped."

Raped? ...Raped?! Her choice of words seems violent and overstated. It was stupid, shameful and humiliating, but not rape. I made a bad mistake. I drank too much. I slept with a guy. I was stupid and ruined my life. But rape? I don't think so.

"Do you know how old this boy was?"

Her words sound far away, like I'm no longer in the room; like I have fallen down inside myself somewhere, far enough that her voice is like a cavernous echo. I try to stay with her. I focus on her question.

"He was a couple years older than me; about sixteen."

"At fourteen, you were a minor and you were under the influence. Even if you didn't say a word, he took advantage of your condition. That is rape."

For 20 years I've called it my fault. For most of that time I didn't even think about it. The first year I couldn't get it out of my mind. I had moments of relief where I laughed at a joke or got sucked into the story on TV, but it always came back. I tried drinking it away, but it only seemed to make it worse. Eventually, I painted it dark colors and hung it on my wall. As time went by I hung up more works of shame and disgust until my wall was covered in it and I became comfortable looking at it every day. It was a childhood room and once I got married I closed that door. Showing Jen around my old room is one thing, but for her to rename the painting rape is a very different thing. The events play through my mind as I try to see it through Jen's eyes.

I'm walking down the hallway to a bedroom. Am I walking? I don't remember walking. Maybe he carried me. I don't remember being carried. *The hallway is narrow. The music is loud. I'm getting scared. The hallway has four doors; three bedroom doors and a bathroom door. Two bedroom doors are shut. One is open and people are sitting around talking and drinking. We are walking toward their parent's bedroom.* Did I walk in the door? I can't remember. *My shirt is being unbuttoned. I'm really scared. I'm standing next to the bed. Then I'm in the bed.* What happened? How did I get in the bed? Did we kiss? Did he take off my clothes? Did I? *His skin is on my skin. He pushes.* I can't think about this anymore. I'm done. Done! I don't know what happened. Jen stands up.

"I'll be right back."

She walks out of the room. I look at the whiteboard. The words are scribbled across the timeline and it's blurry like my mind. It seems far away. I'm falling inside myself. It's a dark hole where I don't feel anything. Jen walks into the room and I try to crawl back out. She's holding a brown fur blanket. She walks to me and lays it over my shoulders, like a shawl. It's heavy and warm. The sensation drags me back to this room. It's so comfortable.

"This is a shame cloak."

The shawl suddenly feels heavier. My emotions are being prodded out of their hiding places. I try to keep them silent.

"When women are sexually abused they tend to blame themselves. This causes a blanket of shame that covers them and every aspect of their lives. Some women may consciously be aware of the shame, but many don't realize the blanket is even there. They just carry the shame with them everywhere they go and it interferes with their work, their relationships, their self-esteem and their spirituality. How does it feel to have this shame cloak on your shoulders?"

"It's heavy."

"What else?"

I've disconnected. All the feelings I tried to pry out of my heart are now in a pile in the bottom of a closet, and I shut the door. My thoughts are stripped of emotion as they drift in and out the window. I'm struggling to mentally stay in the office and listen to Jen. I didn't do anything to stop this guy. I liked him before it happened. I thought he was cute. I didn't say anything. How could he know I didn't want him to do that? I want to let myself drift out of Jen's office window and leave her mentally, but I need to stay here. I can't run away anymore. I grasp for a word that conveys some feeling.

"It feels dark."

"Good. What else?"

I wasn't attacked. I wasn't in a dark alley. He didn't have a weapon. We were just in a house and then in a bedroom. He was drunk, too. We didn't talk. We were just there. I'm sure he saw me look at him earlier that night. He knew I liked him. The more I look for feelings, the harder the images are to get out of my head.

He's pushing himself back and forth on me. Tears stream down the side of my face. I'm silent. I don't speak. The pain is piercing. My head is bumping the headboard. With each push it beats harder and humiliation washes over me. He stops. Relief. The piercing pain subsides. He puts his arms around my waist and pulls me down the bed. He moves around and starts again. The pain is worse, like someone has sprinkled salt on a wound. It's never ending. It's excruciating. I can't take it anymore. My head hits the board again and again and again.

I should have said something, anything. I should have said no, or struggled, or just got up and left. Why didn't I try to leave? Was I that drunk? I can't remember.

Jen is waiting for me to talk more. I want a drink. I want to wash away my thoughts. I'm so tired of fighting the cravings. I want to go home and crawl into bed…for a long time, maybe forever. Jen is still waiting. I try to put my thoughts into words.

"I feel depressed, worthless."

Jen doesn't say anything. She waits.

"I want to crawl into a hole. I don't want to be here anymore."

Jen waits. There is silence, but I don't care. She isn't waiting for me to just talk. She looks like she's listening, but not listening to my words. She's listening to my soul.

"Do you know that this wasn't your fault?"

"No."

"Why do you think it's your fault?"

"Because I was drunk. I didn't try to stop him. I didn't do anything."

"Everyone has a different reaction to sexual assault. Some women fight. Other women freeze. Your body reacts in ways that you can't control. It's the 'Fight or Flight' reaction each of us has for our survival. Do you see that he took advantage of you?"

"He was drunk too. I don't think he knew."

"You don't think he knew what?"

"That I didn't want to do it."

Jen moves around in her chair and leans over close to me with her eyebrows furrowed. She looks frustrated. It's the first time I've seen her like this.

"How old is your son, Andy?"

"He's eleven."

"Think of Andy with someone older who is taking advantage of him."

I feel sick. I try to shove the image out of my mind, but it won't go anywhere. I'm angry. My teeth clench and I want to hit someone.

"Would you blame it on Andy?"

"No!"

"Now, try to see yourself as a young girl. Try to see yourself at Andy's age."

"I was older than Andy."

"You were a child, just like Andy is a child. You probably felt like you were older because you had so much responsibility, but you were still a child."

I picture my son. I try to picture a girl about his size and pretend it's me. I look different than I've imagined. I feel different. I feel like it's someone else, because I've never looked this vulnerable in my own imagination. In my mind I see an innocent girl. I picture her in the bedroom, naked and scared. I feel sorry for her.

"When you see this girl do you blame her for the assault?"

I pause. I know I'm being tricked into feeling sorry for myself. I can't feel sorry for myself. I knew I was on my own. I should have known better. I'm a fighter, a survivor. I can't convince myself that it was his fault. I've never looked at it from an outsider's view. I look so young. I've never pictured myself as a child. In my imagination, I am an older, tougher kid, not this young, innocent child.

130

"No."

"What do you think about her?"

"I feel sorry for her."

"Let's do that. You couldn't have done anything. You may have had a lot of expectations at home, but you couldn't control this. It's an unfair thing that happened to you. It wasn't your fault."

Her words begin to seep into my mind and into the closet where I left my emotions. I want to believe it wasn't entirely my fault, but it seems too easy. I can't quite accept that none of it was my fault, but for the first time I think that maybe I'm not a terrible human being. Maybe I'm not completely worthless.

"You were a victim of a selfish, ruthless boy who took advantage of you. You can take the blame for drinking. But you can't blame yourself for being raped."

My chest tightens. I close my eyes. That word "rape" is so coarse. I still can't completely grasp the idea, but something feels different. I don't feel as lonely. I feel like Jen has made her way in through the locked doors of my heart. I feel a small sense of relief.

"Remember that shame is when we think we are bad because of something that happened to us or something we did. We need to separate ourselves from the events in our life. We all make mistakes and we all have bad things happen to us that are out of our control. We don't define

131

ourselves by these events. We define ourselves by how we deal with them."

I'm staring at the floor. I'm letting her words sink in. They are like cool water in the desert of my heart. I never thought of separating my actions from who I am. When I did something wrong, it confirmed that I was bad. But, I'm not bad. I've done some bad things, but I am not bad. It makes sense. The corner of my mouth turns up slightly into a smile as I can't help feeling a bit of joy and relief that I might be okay, and I don't have to define myself by my past.

Jen stands up and puts her hands on the fur blanket. She lifts it from my shoulders. I want to smile bigger, but I'm afraid to. I'm afraid to think that I'm not bad, because I don't want to find out I'm wrong. I can't disappoint myself. Disappointment hurts so much that I try to force myself not to hope, but I can't help it. Jen puts the cloak down on her office chair.

"I think the Holy Spirit did something inside you today. You are no longer bound by that old shame. You are free."

My self-defense system tries to refuse this wonderful feeling, but I can't. I feel lighter like God lifted me out of the deep well and set me back on the couch in Jen's office. I feel less foggy and more clear-headed. I don't feel a million miles away. I can smell mint from the tea pot on the shelf. I can hear the song from the birds outside the window, and the colors of the pictures on the wall are more vibrant. A voice comes from inside me somewhere. I recognize it. It tries to tell me that I'm a terrible excuse for a human being; that I'm worthless and I'll never amount to anything. It tells me to get up and leave because I'm wasting my time and money. I can do life on my own. I don't need therapy. I just need to stay tough. The voice is familiar, but it's not as loud as usual. It sounds far away and muffled. I'm having a hard time hearing it over my new sense of freedom.

Session 12

I'm driving to Jen's office. My head hurts. My stomach hurts. My chest hurts. If I wasn't so young, I would think I was having a heart attack every time I drove to therapy. I haven't stopped thinking about our last session. I feel unsteady. Last week felt like a miracle as I left the office. Then the word "rape" began to sink in, and the heaviness returned. I turn on the radio. KTIS, a Christian radio station, is on. The guy is singing about trusting God and being protected by him. I thought I trusted God. Maybe I don't. He didn't protect me.

I pull into the parking lot and walk to Jen's office. I turn my neck and pull my shoulders back. I know she'll ask me how I feel. I feel like someone turned my body inside out, and I have no protective skin. I walk into the office.

"Come in."

I go to the couch. I cross my legs and look around the office.

"How was your week?"

I'm looking at the wall and notice I'm biting my nails. I thought about rape all week long. I looked up rape on websites and browsed the bookstore for books. I couldn't get my mind off it. I have so many questions, but I don't want to talk about it, so I lie again, like usual.

"It was fine."

I scramble to think of something else to talk about.

"I went to my first DBT group."

"Great! Tell me about it."

I'm walking down the hall of a church. It's not a typical steeple and pews church. It's a big warehouse type of building. I find a sign that points the way to the DBT room. I walk slowly up to the door. Someone walks by me into the room carrying two chairs. I peer inside. People push two round tables together. Another person carries a lamp with octopus looking arms. Each arm has a different plastic colored lamp shade; blue, yellow, red, green, purple. Someone plugs it in and turns off the bright fluorescent light. The mood in the room changes immediately from stark and sterile to warm and inviting. Candles are placed on the tables and people are talking to each other as they take a seat.

A big, loud blond woman walks around the room hugging everyone. I turn away. She scares me. I sit down in a chair close to Terri, the group leader. Three teenage girls are sitting together. They're all beautiful, but they don't look like they know it. Two of them are talking and laughing. The other one is quiet. She is smiling faintly, but there is deep pain in her eyes; much more than seems possible for a girl her age. Another woman is older than me, maybe in her early fifties. She is talking to someone

135

and her voice is deep and scratchy like she has smoked most of her life.

After everyone is seated, Terri starts our group with a prayer. She then goes through a quick overview of what our group is about, why we're here, and what we're trying accomplish. People are quiet, but I'm not sure we're listening. Our body language exposes our preoccupation with our own thoughts. I'm not sure how many of us are capable of focusing on what someone else is saying. Terri seems to know this from experience and keeps talking. After a quick overview we do a meditation exercise.

She asks us to find an object in the room to focus on. She's going to time us for one minute, and we're to concentrate on the thing we're looking at. Each time another thought pops into our head, we're supposed to dismiss it and go back to the object. I decide to look at the funny octopus lamp. She starts the timer. I'm thinking about the different colors of the lamp. Then I think about the girl next to me molding play-dough in her hands and how that must feel kind of cool, but it's also distracting. I realize I'm not thinking about the lamp. The lamp. I'm staring harder at the lamp and think about my grocery list, and I have to get milk later. The lamp. This book is really thick. I wonder if we're going to get through it all or how there could be so much information in there. I wonder what's in there. The lamp. Think about the lamp. The timer is ticking softly. I don't like the ticking sound. Someone coughs. I hate that. The lamp. Thinking about the lamp. Think about the lamp. The lamp. Maybe if I repeat the word "lamp" I can stay focused. The lamp. The lamp. Someone coughs again. AAHHH! Shut up! I'm mad now. I can't think about the lamp because there's too much noise. No, it's because I can never

136

focus. Why don't I have ADD? I still don't get that. If I had ADD maybe I'd get to play with some play-dough. The cinnamon smell of the candle drifts by. I like the candles. The lamp! I keep forgetting about the lamp. How can anyone think about one thing for a whole minute! I can't think about it for more than a couple of seconds! There are way too many thoughts going through my mind. Does everyone have this many thoughts? The timer dings. Time is up. We go around the group and talk about our meditation time. I'm comforted by the fact that everyone seemed to have trouble focusing on one object. Some people got off track and never came back to their object at all. Maybe I'm not the worst one after all. Maybe I did better than everyone else! Ugh. Why does everything turn into a competition for me? I hope we don't really have to do that every week.

I look at Jen.

"It was ok. She gave us these huge workbooks and talked about dialectics and something about how opposites can work together."

"Yes. That's a big concept."

"Yeah. It was very hard to understand. She used an idea to explain it to us. She said, 'I love you guys right where you are, AND I love you guys enough to want you to have a better life.' She said dialectics is understanding that two thoughts like those can co-exist. We all disagreed, because if she loves us right where we are, then there's no reason for us to change. If she wants us to change, then she can't love us right where we're at. It doesn't make any sense."

I start getting mad just thinking about it. I feel like I have a palette of paints with all the colors neatly separated and Terri mixed them all up. My heart is beating fast. Jen smiles like she knows something I don't.

"How would you describe how you feel right now?"

"Irritable."

"Why do you think you feel irritable?"

I shift around on the couch. I look out the window. I really don't want to answer her question.

"I don't know."

"We've dug up a lot of emotion lately."

"Yeah."

"How do you feel you are dealing with it?"

"Well, I guess I'm having a hard time with it."

I feel sleepy. Emotions are draining, and they wear me out fast.

"What do you think is the hardest thing for you?"

I think about a conversation I had with Nancy during the week.

We're walking through a park. We talk about me. That's all we talk about because that's all I can think about. My

138

recovery has lasted months, and I can't think of anything else.

"Did you have a good session with Jen this week?"

I pause. How do I begin to tell her what we talked about?

"It was hard."

"What was hard about it?"

"We talked about something that happened to me when I was pretty young."

My head hurts. I can't talk about this. I feel squeamish. I feel like something is crawling all over me. But, I have to talk about it. She is safe. She is more than safe. God has used her in amazing ways that I can't explain, like the time I was mad at God because I couldn't justify my drinking anymore so I tested him by saying, "If you really don't want me to drink anymore just say so and have Nancy call me before I get my alcohol out of the garage." Nancy and I weren't even friends back then. She was my Bible study leader, and she called everyone in our group once a week. She had just called me the day before so I knew she wasn't going to call me today. Giving God this chance to stop me helped me justify my drinking again. But as I reached for the garage door, the phone rang. Goose bumps raised the hair straight up off my arms and neck. For two more rings I couldn't move. I finally told myself it was just a coincidence; it could be anybody, but as I reached for the phone I saw Nancy's name on the caller I.D. It felt like God was calling me. I was so stunned I told her the whole story and everything about my drinking, and she became my accountability partner

139

after that. I call her an accountability partner, but she's more than that.

I have a voicemail message she left me a few months ago. I feel stupid keeping it, but I can't delete it. All it says is, "Hey, you've gone a little silent on me. Just wondering if you're okay. Talk to you later." I never had anything like that growing up. No one knew if I was silent or hurt or missing. I often stayed out until three in the morning. When I came home everyone was asleep. Sometimes when I feel lonely, I play Nancy's phone message over and over. It helps me feel like I can face the world.

I decide that after all the stuff she's gone through with me if I can't tell her about the deeper things in my life now, I never will. I try to find the words. It's hard to breathe. I feel like there's a strap around my chest that was buckled too tight.

"Can you tell me about it?"

I need to say something. My mind is swirling. I have to talk even if it doesn't make sense.

"I called it a really bad mistake.... Jen called it...rape."

Saying the word sucks the life out of me, and I want to sit down and melt into the ground.

"Wow, so you were raped?"

"I guess so."

"How old were you?"

"Fourteen."

"What do you mean you guess so?"

"Because I was drunk... I didn't try to get away...I didn't really do anything."

"Maybe you don't want to call it rape because you would have to admit that you were a victim."

I stare straight ahead. I don't understand.

"Being an alcoholic is not being a victim. The alcoholic makes the choice to drink. Your husband and kids are the victims. I'm not saying it isn't hard on you, but as an alcoholic, you are causing the wreckage. As a rape victim, you had no control. I don't think you want to admit that you were in a situation where you didn't have control."

She's right. I can feel it. If I admitted I was raped, I would be admitting that something happened to me. And I would be admitting that it could happen again. If I call it a mistake of my own, I'm still in control, and I can control whether it could happen again. I hate the idea that something could happen to me that I can't control.

This seems like an important thing to talk about so I tell Jen about my talk with Nancy.

"I was talking to my friend this week and she said something that made sense. She said maybe my problem is I don't want to admit that I wasn't in control. Like, if the rape was my fault, then maybe I could keep it from happening again."

"That's very insightful."

"Yeah, that's what I thought."

Jen stands up, grabs a dry erase marker and draws a line straight down the center of the white board.

"I want you to make two lists. On one list, write down all the things in your life that you have control over. On the other list, write down all the things in your life that you don't have any control over."

I make a line down the center of the paper and quickly write on the top of the page "Control" and "No control." She continues to explain.

"For instance, you can control whether you get out of bed in the morning, right?"

"Right."

"Write that down."

I start writing.

"What's something you don't have any control over?"

I think about things that happen in my life during the day. I look out the window. Rain is drizzling down the glass.

"The weather. I can't control the weather."

"That's true. Write that down."

I write down "Weather" on the "No control" side.

"What else?"

I'm stuck. I can't think of anything.

"What is something that makes you angry?"

I think. That shouldn't be hard to come up with.

"When the phone rings and it's someone I don't want to talk to."

"Can you control if someone calls you?"

"No."

"Can you control if you answer the phone?"

"…Yes."

Jen tells me to write that down and I do, but I've drifted somewhere else. The idea of not answering the phone is like the clouds parting on a rainy day and the sun shining on my face. How could it never occur to me that I don't have to answer my own phone? I quickly write down on my paper "Phone call" on the "No control" side and "Answer the phone" on the "Control" side. I feel a new sense of freedom, like Jen unlocked the padlock that chained me to the phone. I wonder what other things I'm chained to that I don't know about.

"The list we are making is providing boundaries for you. It's going to help you see the reality of what we can control and what we can't. Kids from alcoholic homes grow up without any boundaries resulting in chaos. Chaos makes people feel like they have to control everything around them in order to stop the chaos, but it's impossible to control everything and everyone around you. Everyone needs to feel in control of their life. By placing boundaries, you can release the things you can't control and will feel better about the things you can control. I'd like you to bring that home and add as many things to the list as you can."

"Ok."

I feel much lighter as I walk out of Jen's office thinking about the possibilities. As I climb into my van I look across the road at the Harley dealership. It's the first time I haven't felt the urge to ride away from my life.

Session 13

I'm sitting in Jen's office on the couch.

"How was your week?"

"It was fine."

Automatic response. It wasn't fine. My week was weird. Every week is weird. And hard. Recovery and therapy feels like paddling up stream in stormy weather with one arm tied behind my back.

"What did you learn in the DBT group this week?"

"We're talking about the Wise Mind; combining logic with emotion and the reasons we need to use both in order to make good decisions."

"What did you learn?"

"Well, I thought because I don't like to share my emotions or feelings that I would be logical. But I really don't make very logical decisions. I make emotional decisions. So, I don't know. It's confusing."

"There is a lot of information so just take it a little at a time."

"We also talked about using skills in order to keep us from drinking or whatever self-destructive behavior each of us has."

I was a little surprised to find the variety of destructive behaviors in our group. I imagined a bunch of alcoholics, but there's a girl who cuts herself, and a girl who can't function because of her anxiety. It's not just anxiety like I see in my friends when a big event is coming up. This person can hardly function without someone telling her what to do.

"What kind of skills are you learning?"

"Well, my running falls under two different skill categories; 'reducing vulnerability' and 'distraction'. It reduces my vulnerability to rage and drinking, and I can use it as a distraction if I'm angry or have a craving. In Dr. Nelson's office I learned that it may also help reduce my obsessive thoughts."

"That's great."

I think of my recovery meeting when someone asked, "How do you know if you're an alcoholic if you can go a long time, even months without drinking?" The response was that if you're an alcoholic, even if you don't drink, you'll be obsessed with thoughts of drinking. A regular drinker doesn't obsess about whether they are an alcoholic or not. It makes me think about my running. Dr. Nelson said I don't need to run more than 35 minutes in order to get the mental benefits from running. After that I'm just wearing out my body or asking for an injury. I made the mistake of telling Nancy about Dr. Nelson's recommendation. She's been questioning me about my running ever since. I know she doesn't understand. Her brain isn't wired like mine. My mind is like a motor that never stops. It's like a car without neutral. There's just forward and reverse and the gas pedal is stuck to the floor. There's no key to turn off. I hit the brakes, but the tires just spin in place. I can't make it stop.

In outpatient treatment, we were told that many alcoholics transfer their addiction from one thing to another. At least running isn't hurting anyone. Maybe I spend time away from my family while I'm running, but I'm supposed to have some hobbies or things that make me feel good about myself. JB and I fight about it sometimes because I stay out too long and he gets worried, but that's not my problem. He and Nancy are a lot alike. I don't know why I'm drawn to them. They're both so logical. They don't understand people like me. I'm passionate and persistent and driven to push myself. I just want to be somebody. I don't know why I let these guys have so much influence in my life. I think I believe that they might be able to help me find the off switch to my brain.

Jen switches the subject.

"Did you work on your list of things you can and can't control?"

"Yes, I did."

It feels like a great time to change the subject. I rummage through my bag for my notebook. I get out my list. Jen looks at me with expectation. I start reading.

"I can't control what I did in the past. I can control what I'm doing today. I can't control what JB says to me. I can control how I react to it. I can't control my kids' behavior. I can control my own behavior. I can't control…"

I pause as my eyes glance over the next item. I didn't realize how much emotion this would bring up. I take a deep breath. I try to shove the images out of my mind from my journaling last night, but they are so strong.

"I can't control what happened in my childhood. I can control how I raise my own children."

I'm silent, grasping mentally for something to hang on to. A lump in my throat is the only thing between my stoicism and tears. I've done a lot of journaling since I went to treatment, but last night was different. Instead of putting my thoughts on paper, I was reading the story as my hands did the writing, like I was just an observer.

I'm sitting in my office. The kids are in bed. I've been wrestling with the unfairness of my childhood. I've finally been able to share with Jen what my life was like, but I still don't feel good. I'm still mad. I still feel like I can't get over how unfair it is. I still want someone to turn the clock back so we can do it over. I still want my dad to come home after work and kiss my mom. I still want to have dinner together at the table where we all sit and talk to each other. I still want to have a bed time. I still want to have chores and allowance and consequences. I still want to be held when my heart hurts.

I read something in my recovery literature about stages of grief. I always thought of grief as something that happens after someone dies. It never occurred to me that I could grieve things other than death, like grieving the fact that I can never drink again. Jen told me that I haven't grieved the loss of my childhood and that I won't be able to let it go until I go through all the stages. I think I'm finally willing to try. I've always resisted grief in the past because grief is sad, and I didn't want to be sad. I thought it was easier to stay angry, but being angry has taken up too much of my energy, and it causes me to be someone I don't want to be. The problem is I don't know how to begin to grieve. Maybe if I can picture in my head what it looks like to lose my childhood. It's always easier for me to understand a concept if I can visualize it.

I begin to write everything that comes to mind. There's a hill with one tree on top and a forest of trees below. I'm walking up the hill. The whole area is covered in a thick fog. I'm dressed in green army clothes. I have a gun slung over my back and a hard hat on my head. As I walk up the hill I see that I'm on a battlefield. It's quiet. The stillness is eerie. Then I see them. There are bodies lying all over the ground right where they fell during battle. I begin walking toward the closest body. Though death is everywhere, there is peace all around me, like I'm standing on holy ground.

As I get closer to the body I'm surprised by its size. I stop and stare as I realize it's a child's body. My heart begins to ache at the thought of a child being killed in battle. The child's body is face down. Long blond hair hints that it's a girl. And then I begin to put the pieces together. I move closer to see her face. I know who she is. The tears come fast and fall down my cheeks. I try to catch my breath as I see that God has led me straight to my own battlefield. The little girl is me and the battlefield is my childhood. I kneel down beside her broken body. I can't hold back the enormous wave of emotion that is crashing down on me. I

149

pick her up in my arms and rock her back and forth, something I know she always wanted.

I stop writing. I curl up in a ball and sob. It's such uncontrolled sobbing that I finally run out of energy to cry. I want to go to bed, but there is more to write. I lay the body down on the ground and pick up a shovel nearby. I start digging her grave. With each shovel full of dirt I think of who this girl represents. She was the little girl who wanted to be taken care of. She was innocent and naïve and desperately wanted to be held and hugged and touched and comforted. She was the girl on the bus whose favorite hat was ruined. She was the girl alone in the woods with questions left unanswered. She was the girl in her bed hiding from the shouting and things breaking outside her bedroom door. As much as I want to change everything and save her from the pain, I can't. I can only grieve for her. I pick her up and hold her again and cry some more. Then I gently lay her body in the grave. Her little body is so much smaller than I remember. Another figure appears and is walking toward the grave. I know right away who it is. Jesus stands at the graveside with me looking at the little body. Tears run down his cheeks too. We wait a moment. Then I scoop a shovel full of dirt. Reluctantly, I turn the handle of the shovel letting the dirt fall lightly into the hole. Jesus picks up a shovel and we both work silently together.

There are several other bodies each one representing something lost. One is the little girl who wanted to be beautiful for her dad. She died to be the son she thought her dad wanted. Another one is the girl who wanted a social life with friends and sleepovers. She died to keep the secrets of her family and take care of her younger siblings. Another is a girl with self-worth, a good student,

150

pure and innocent. She died when she was raped and covered her pain with her drinking. I hold each little girl while Jesus stands beside me. We don't talk. He just waits with me and helps me dig the holes. As we bury the last little body, I sense that He grieves their childhood even more than I do. I'm exhausted now and covered in dirt and tears. I lay down my shovel and sit against the tree. Jesus sits next to me, and we sit quietly looking at all the dirt piles. There's nothing to say, only feel.

Jen is quiet. She is good at sensing my emotions. Maybe because I shut down when I get emotional.

"I did some journaling last night about my childhood."

Jen is still quiet. She's listening and waiting. I love how she waits. She's the only person who ever waits quietly for me to find the courage somewhere inside myself to talk.

"I understand things better when I can see a picture. While I was journaling I could see a picture in my mind of my childhood. I thought grief was just for when someone dies. I guess I had to see some of my dreams actually die in order to feel sad about them."

A smile turns the corner of her mouth up slightly. It's all the confirmation I need that I'm alright. I feel like I'm standing on the middle of a teeter-totter, trying to keep it balanced. On the one side I'm still protecting myself, making sure I don't get hurt again. On the other side I'm working on finding and sharing my feelings and allowing myself to take off my protective covering. The cool air of criticism and abandonment seems to blow every time I'm unprotected, so I cling tightly to my shell looking for any hint that I may be let down or hurt or disappointed. But with Jen, I never feel that way. She is so accepting. I just can't let go of my fear that somehow, some day she is going to disappoint me, too.

Session 14

I'm anxious to get to Jen's office. I had the worst dream of my life, and I can't get it out of my mind.

I'm in my van with my kids and two of their friends. We go off a bridge and land in the water. As the van starts to sink, I go into action. Usually in my dreams everything is in slow motion, and the faster I need to go, the slower I feel my feet moving. This time is different. I'm thinking about what I have to do to get everyone out of the van, and it's working. The water rises quickly, but I'm unfastening seat belts and pushing kids out the side door just as fast. By the last child, the van is almost entirely underwater, and I'm worried about getting him out in time to breathe. I don't fumble at all. Everything I'm doing is quick and graceful. The seat belt unlatches easily, and I grab the last child and swim out the door and to the surface. Relief washes over me, as we all bob in the water. I can't believe we got out so fast. And then I see him. Andy is in the back seat looking out the window at me. How did I miss him? Only the back windows are visible above the water now. I panic, but Andy doesn't. He looks calm, almost serene. Water begins filling the back of the van where he is sitting. It quickly rises over his chest to his head, past his mouth and within moments he is under. His expression never changes. As the back end of the van begins to go under, he raises his hand and waves to me. He has a reassuring look on his face as if to tell me it's ok,

153

don't worry. He has accepted his fate. The corners of his mouth turn up into the slightest smile. He is saying goodbye. And then the van is gone.

I wake up panicked thinking I've lost my son. I sit up in bed. I'm crying. I go to Andy's room and open the door quietly. I'm afraid to look. Realistically, I know he's going to be there, but my gut is telling me to be afraid. I push the door open and peek my head inside. His brown hair is sticking out from underneath the blankets. I watch the blanket rise and fall with his breathing. He's fine. It was just a dream. I step inside so I can see his face. He's only eleven years old, but he seems older. He seems more mature than that. I've made him grow up too fast. I know how he feels. My parents did it to me, and I swore I wouldn't do it to my kids! I walk out of his room because I don't want to wake him up.

I think I probably had the dream as a result of Andy's play therapy. I worry about him. He's been in play therapy for a few months now and sometimes we're not sure if he's getting any better. It's hard to tell. For the most part, he seems normal. In play therapy, he plays with action figures like he does at home. Sometimes we wonder if it's worth the money, but then his therapist explains to us what his playing means and it makes sense. Our hope for him is renewed, and we continue to believe that this will help him deal with the issues he's going through. Last week during our parent meeting with Samantha, we told her how he's been acting out at home and fighting more with his sister, Jenna. We were surprised when she told us that was a great sign. He wouldn't fight with his sister if he didn't feel comfortable with our parenting. It's amazing how difficult things make sense with the right perspective.

I get to Jen's office right on time. She invites me in and I sit on the couch. I'm thinking about the dream again. I can't get it out of my mind.

"How are you?"

"I'm ok."

I say I'm ok, but I'm not even trying to hide the fact that I'm not ok. Jen can tell something is up.

"What's going on?"

I tell Jen about the dream. I leave out some of the details so I don't cry.

"When did you have this dream?"

"A couple of days ago."

"And it's still bothering you?"

"I'm worried about Andy. He seems really depressed."

"What does his therapist say?"

"She said during play therapy, he'd get worse before he gets better because he will have to move through his emotions, and that will be the hard part."

"So, maybe he is working through that now."

"Yeah, probably."

"I'm sure that will be hard for you, too."

"Yeah."

"That's probably what your dream is about. It's hard to watch your children go through pain. But you are not losing him. You are helping him heal. I'm sure Samantha is watching his progress, but if you get worried about him let Samantha know how you feel. You are a better judge of his emotions than anyone else."

I'm not sure I'm a better judge or maybe I would have noticed what kind of damage I was doing all these years. Maybe I would have seen the reflection of my anger and unpredictable behavior in his eyes. I think about Andy's eyes. Jenna's eyes are huge and beautiful, but Andy's are deep and full of secrets. He internalizes everything around him and keeps it there to think and ponder and solve. Everything I throw at Jenna and Johnny, they throw back at me, but Andy accepts it and owns it and tries to do something with it. Whether it's his personality or that he's the first born, he seems to have taken on all of my problems. If I can't handle them at the age of 34, I can only imagine how he is trying to deal with them at eleven. I guess that's what the twitching is about.

"Are you still running every day?"

"Most days."

"Is that helping with your emotions?"

"Sometimes."

"How come?"

"Sometimes I run and I feel great. Other times I run and it makes me madder than when I started."

"Why do you think you get mad?"

"It feels like sometimes I can't go fast enough or far enough, so I feel like a loser."

"How far is enough?"

I think about it. It's like my thirst for alcohol. There is never enough to quench the thirst. The more I take, the more I want. Maybe Nancy's right. Maybe I've just traded addictions. I hate it when she's right.

"It's really never enough."

Jen's eyes soften. I didn't know they could get any softer.

"Let's go into the play room."

Jen stands up and I follow her. I love the play room. We haven't been in there in a while and I feel calmer just thinking about it. I can't call it fun, because it's still hard to talk about what we're doing in there, but at least it's easier to process when we're moving around and using toys and objects. We walk through the waiting room and into the play room.

"Why don't you choose some objects from the wall to put in the sand tray that represent how you feel when you run?"

I go to the wall. It's easier this time than the first day we were here. I don't feel the pressure. I think about running. I pick up a skinny female figure. Then I grab some fences. I look around at all the other toys and decide I have enough. I line up the fences the long way through the sand tray so there's a lane down the center. I put the skinny female doll in the middle between the fences on the lane.

"You didn't choose much."

"No. Nothing else seems right."

"So, what do the fences represent?"

I have to think. I'm not sure why I grabbed them exactly. I just felt like they were the right thing to grab.

"I don't know."

"Fences usually represent boundaries. Running can be healthy for you if you're running for your health. If you can never go far enough, maybe you aren't doing it for your health. Can you think of another reason you run?"

I look at the wood trim on the floor along the baseboard. I follow it with my eyes to the corner.

"I'm competitive. I like to win."

"Do you run races?"

"No."

"So, what are you trying to win?"

"I don't know. I like to run alone."

"Why do you think you like to run alone?"

I think about the few times I've run with a friend or neighbor. I feel my body tense.

"When I run with other people it's not relaxing at all. I feel really tense and anxious."

"Why do you think you feel that way?"

I look at the floor again searching the corner of the room for an answer or an escape from these questions.

"I feel like I have to keep up with them or be faster than them. I'm always worried about our pace. I'm worried I'm slowing them down."

My stomach sinks. Running might not make me happy, but I don't want anyone telling me what to do. I already gave up drinking. I'm not giving up running.

"What do you think would be a reasonable boundary for your running?"

"When I saw Dr. Nelson, he had said that running 35 minutes is enough to release dopamine, which is what I need."

"What do you think about sticking with 35 minutes?"

"It makes me feel anxious."

"Would you be willing to try?"

I breathe in deep. I look at the wall. I feel confined. I feel the need to run out of the room again. I hate this. But I don't feel like I have any choice. I don't feel like I've had choices for years.

"I guess so."

"It might help you find some of the balance you need in your life."

I hate the word balance. I've heard it a million times. When I think of that word it reminds me of a Bible verse I read once about God liking people that are hot or cold, but the luke-warm people he spits out. Balance sounds luke-warm to me. There's no passion in balance. Without passion, there's boredom and hopelessness and depression. I feel like this guy I saw on the T.V. show, *Ripley's Believe it or Not*. This tall, skinny man crawled into this tiny little box by twisting and turning his legs and arms all over the place. He climbed into the box at the beginning of the show and stayed there until the end of the show. I was getting claustrophobic just watching him. I feel like that now. Like everyone is trying to fit me into a box and shut the lid. I can't do it! I'm suffocating just thinking about it.

Session 15

I'm almost to Jen's office. I drive past the Harley Dealership. I really shouldn't be driving this way anymore, because the temptation to buy a motorcycle and run away is almost as strong as the temptation to drink. I was justifying my reasons for escaping until my friend, Ann set me straight. I've known Ann as long as I've known Nancy. If Nancy is a mentor, parent figure in my life, Ann feels like a big sister. Ann is six-feet tall, and strikingly beautiful, which can be intimidating when she's not smiling. My first memory of Ann was three years ago when I was standing in a room of 30 women for a Bible study. I was about to perform a skit. My hands were shaking, and I thought I was going to throw up. Ann was part of the Women's Ministry team which I had newly joined. She was sitting in the second row and just before I started my presentation she gave me a huge, reassuring smile. I felt a surge of confidence and performed my skit flawlessly. I continued helping out with the Bible study, and Ann and I became good friends. She was fun to work with because her administrative, structured-style provided a great sounding board for my creative, unstructured ideas. After I got out of treatment I realized I had three different kinds of friends. There were friends who I didn't talk to very much after treatment. There were friends who helped our family by bringing a meal, helping me clean or watching my kids. And then there were the friends who I leaned on. Ann was one of the friends I leaned on. She sat on the phone with me for hours when my depression was at its worst. Often there was nothing to say so she just sat quietly on the other end of the line letting me know she was there. She did more than her share of driving me to my outpatient meetings, and she even bought my kids' school supplies while I was in the hospital, and JB was too shocked to function well.

I wrote Ann an e-mail about some of my frustration with recovery hoping to get some sympathy.

I am frustrated with all this work I am doing. I never feel like I'm getting anywhere. I just want a list of things I need to do to get out of this nightmare and return to normal life, but there doesn't seem to be a list, just endless amounts of emotional hurdles. I'm tired of trying to stop running after my 35 minutes are up. I'm tired of trying to tell JB how I FEEL about everything. And I'm tired of driving back and forth to DBT group to meditate and practice being non-judgmental with myself and learning how to accept all the crap that has gone on in my life. What if I don't want to accept it?! What if I think people should be held accountable for their mistakes?! I've been working on this stuff for so long. I'm sick of it! And why do I have to do all the work? Why didn't my parents do it right in the first place? JB isn't perfect. Why doesn't he work on something for a while? I am just one decision away from trading in my minivan for a Harley and riding off into the sunset.

One of the reasons I love Ann is because of her brutal honesty as she proved in her reply e-mail.

If you don't want to hear an honest answer to your statements, then don't continue to read this e-mail. If I

162

was there right now, I'd slap you. Look how far you've come! Remember why you're doing this? Your kids need you. Your husband needs you. Driving off on a Harley is selfish. You are not a quitter, and I'm not willing to stand by while you throw it all away!

I stare at the computer screen. I feel like I've just been run over by a truck.

As I walk into Jen's office, Ann's words are imbedded in my mind and rather than feel sorry for myself, I feel a new resolve to keep working toward being the mom I need to be. It doesn't always feel good, but it's nice to have friends that kick me in the butt when I need it.

Jen's office is warm, as usual. Not just warm as in temperature. The colors are warm. The light is warm. The chairs are warm. Jen's eyes are warm. They are so warm I want to climb inside them and sleep. I want to be little again. I don't want to be an adult. I don't want to be married. I don't want to have kids. I'm a failure, and I should have thought of that before I tried to create a life around me full of relationships that I was going to ruin. I don't know why society hasn't made some kind of testing process before allowing people to be parents. Why would God do this to us? Why would He build us to need relationships, and then leave us to hurt each other?

Jen is sitting in her chair.

"So, how are you?"

She says it with enthusiasm. She has a lot of energy, but some days she has more energy than others. This is one of those energetic days. It's annoying.

163

"I'm fine."

"What did you work on this week?"

I don't have to think long because I'm so irritable I can't sit still.

"Running."

"Were you able to keep the running within your boundaries?"

"No."

"Why not?"

"I usually run this 5-mile loop. In order to stick to 35 minutes, I had to stop at 17 ½ minutes and turn around. I felt like I was giving up by turning back instead of running my 5-mile route."

"Why do you think you feel that way?"

"It's like if I stop early, I'm quitting. If I quit, I'm a quitter. If I'm a quitter, I'm a loser."

We're both quiet. I'm done talking. I think she's waiting for me to go on, but I don't have anything else to say.

"Why do you think you're a loser if you don't run the whole thing?"

"Because… I feel like a failure."

"What are you afraid of failing?"

"Life. It's not just running. It's like my running is tied to everything else. If I settle for 35 minutes in running, I'll settle for anything. I'll settle for doing an average job. I'll settle for being an average mom or an average wife or an average friend or an average Christian."

"What's wrong with being average?"

My body freezes. I can't move. My brain has been jolted. I can't think. I heard the words that came out of her mouth, but I can't figure out what she said. I always think we are on the same page. I think we're playing the same game until she comes up with a perspective that tells me we are miles apart from each other. No wonder life is hard. We don't all play with the same rules. I don't understand why she thinks that average is good enough. Does she really think average is okay? Does she think that it's okay for me to be average because I'm in therapy? Maybe, since I'm in therapy and I'm a recovering alcoholic and I have depression I can't live an above-average life.

"Adult children of alcoholics don't learn to separate their behavior from who they are. They learn that if they make a mistake, they are a mistake. You need to begin to separate who you are from what you do. You are not your behavior."

What she says sounds familiar. Foreign, but familiar.

"I think Terri talked about that in our DBT group. She was trying to explain something, but we weren't getting it. We were talking about mindfulness. Something about just observing or something."

"Yes! It's all about experiencing and living in the moment, while ignoring the part of you that wants to judge yourself. You have to learn to observe things without judging them."

I look at her, but I'm not really looking at her. I'm still thinking about whether being average is okay. I was raised with perfection. Our house was a wreck, but my dad worked on everything until it was perfect.

I'm 10 years old. We're going to my cousin's house. It's about an hour-and-a-half away. I'm really excited. They have a cool log cabin house and lots of land. We play in the woods and drive their jeep and four-wheeler around. We play hide and seek and build forts. We were supposed to leave a couple hours ago, but my dad is cleaning out his van. He doesn't just clean it; he takes every single thing he has out of the van, carpet rolls, tool boxes, jackets, blankets, crates, cans, boards. He has a small village in the back of his van. Once he takes everything out, he puts it back in like a puzzle. Everything seems to have a place and if he puts it in the wrong place, he takes it out again and reorganizes it. We aren't allowed in the van until every tool and box and crate and piece of carpet are perfectly placed. My brothers and I go play, because we know it will be a long time before we actually leave.

I guess it was more than just perfection with my dad. It was an obsession or compulsion. He did this with everything from his office to the garage. No wonder he drank. If he was that obsessive about having things in order and our house was trashed, that had to make him slightly insane. For a moment, I'm standing in his shoes as he comes home from work, and I understand why he might have screamed and yelled every night when he went

166

from his highly organized work environment to our house of chaos.

Sometimes he tried to show us how to do something. He'd start by letting us help him with a project, but we could never do it right, so we were set aside while he finished it. Or more likely, he took apart whatever we had started and did it over. I'm beginning to see the reason that nothing I do is good enough. I've adopted my dad's perfectionism. I don't know how to get rid of it. It's ingrained in me like rocks in cement. I feel like if I let go of it, I will fall apart, because nothing will be holding me together.

"When you run this week, try to observe your surroundings without judging yourself. Ok?"

"Ok."

"In order to grow, you're going to make some mistakes. You have to give yourself room to make mistakes. You need to forgive yourself, be kind to yourself, and give yourself some space. When you are able to become a friend to yourself and not be judgmental, then you will start to be effective."

Being nonjudgmental and kind to myself feels wrong. I feel like if I let myself off the hook I'll never get any better. It's the competitiveness inside me that drives me to be better and better. There's no second place. There is only winning and losing. If I'm not judgmental with myself, where do I draw the line? What if I drank again? Would that be okay? Can I be nonjudgmental about relapsing? It feels like Jen is trying to wrestle this competitiveness out of my hands. If I lose this fight I'm

167

worried I won't know who I am anymore. It feels like being strapped to a table for a lobotomy, and if I don't fight it off I'll never be the same. The only reason I'm still here listening is because of my kids. If I had any idea about how to stay sober on my own, I would be out of here. Jen continues talking about DBT skills.

"Being effective means to see a situation for what it is and react to it in a way that benefits you and others."

"So, right now I'm not effective because when something happens, my reaction is to explode or judge myself into another bad situation."

"Yes!"

My sweet, logical husband tried to explain something like this to me once, but I got mad at him. Now that I'm hearing the same message from Jen, it hits me that banging my head against the wall isn't going to change anything other than the wall and my head. We talked about this in treatment too, but in a little different way. If we have a craving, we need to play the tape all the way through. In other words, I have to think further out than the drink and think about what the consequences are after I've taken the first drink. If I can think it all the way through, I can usually talk myself out of the drink because it's not worth the negative results. But it takes practice to remember that when I'm in the middle of a craving, and I want the drink really bad and I'm not thinking, only feeling.

"So what kind of thoughts could you use to be more effective in your running?"

I look up at the ceiling. I feel like a little kid staying after class to learn something I was too dumb to understand during class. I close my eyes and start tapping my foot trying to think of something, but I'm frustrated, which makes it hard to think. Jen gives me some help.

"What if you told yourself that running for 35 minutes is good enough?"

"What if I don't believe that?"

"Fake it 'til you make it."

Jen says this with gusto, like a cheerleader. I hate cheerleaders. Not personally, I just don't like the cheering thing. I think she can tell that I'm annoyed, so she begins to lay it out piece by piece.

"Your emotions follow your thoughts. You don't feel something until you think of something. So, if you fill your mind with positive thoughts, you can trick yourself into feeling good."

I'm staring at her. I feel defensive right now and I'm not sure why.

"Let's try an example. Right now you look a little annoyed. Is that right?"

I don't want her to think I'm annoyed with her, but it must be obvious.

"Yes."

"Ok, right now your face is giving this away. I want you to just slightly smile. It doesn't have to be big, just turn up the corners of your mouth."

Everything in me is fighting against this request. I tell myself to turn up the corners of my mouth whether I feel like it or not. I have to consciously force myself to do it. I turn up one corner of my mouth and it's weird, but I can't smile, even the slightest little bit, without feeling a little happier. It's like my face and my feelings are directly connected.

"How do you feel?"

I want to tell her I'm still annoyed. Why am I fighting myself to stay mad instead of letting myself feel happy?

"It is working. I feel better."

"Good. So if you can force yourself to say that running 35 minutes is good enough, you might actually begin to feel that it is enough."

I'm afraid. I'm afraid that if I think it is good enough and really believe it then everything will be good enough and I won't stand out or be better than anyone else or count for anything. No one will notice me, and I can't let myself go unnoticed. It adds to my loneliness.

"Have you been communicating with JB?"

"Sort of."

I think about the homework I'm supposed to do with him. I'm supposed to tell him how I feel once a day. I usually wait until the last moment of the day.

JB and I are in bed watching TV. My homework for therapy is to tell him one feeling word. I don't want to tell him anything. I want to go to sleep and not wake up. I take a deep breath. What do I feel? I feel anxious for sure. I could say that. Ok, I'll say that. ... I want to tell him, but I'm scared. What if he's not listening? What will he say? He probably thinks this is so stupid. Why can't I just say it! I wait for a commercial. I turn to him and say,

"I'm supposed to tell you how I feel."

He turns away from the TV and looks at me. He looks confused. He turns off the TV.

"Ok."

"You know, for therapy, I'm supposed to tell you how I feel at least once a day."

"I didn't know that."

I'm messing this up. I didn't start very well.

"Well, yeah, I'm supposed to tell you how I feel so I can start figuring out how I feel and communicate with you."

"...what do you want me to say?"

"I don't know yet. Just hang on."

I breathe again.

171

"Tonight I feel anxious."

"Why do you feel anxious?"

His eyebrows are raised and he looks defensive. I didn't want to say more than that. I'm done.

"I don't know. I'm just saying it. You don't have to say anything."

"Ok."

He looks at me to be sure that's all he needs to say. I wish he would just watch TV again. I hate this. What's he supposed to say? I feel like a little kid.

He looks like he's about to break something. I think he is. It's like we're both trying to fit pieces of my porcelain vase back together after it was destroyed in my childhood. The pieces are fragile and delicate and I don't know exactly where they go. I wanted to put it back together myself, but I'm supposed to let him help me. So I'm trying to let him help me. I'm just afraid he'll break something.

"How did you communicate with him?"

"I told him how I felt one night."

"Wow! That is big! Do you get that? That is a big step!"

I smile slightly. I don't want to smile too wide. It always surprises me when she gets excited about something I did. It feels good. But I don't want to get too comfortable. I'm always waiting for the "but" statement to explain the things I didn't do right, but they never come. I feel proud

172

now that I shared. I feel brave. It sounds silly when I think of it. But I still feel like I did a good job, like it was good enough.

Session 16

Andy has been in play therapy for a while now, but we're to a turning point and it's getting hard for me. His play therapist, Samantha, told us that kids start working through their issues by playing with inanimate objects like trucks or blocks. These things represent the furthest thing from emotions. As the child feels more comfortable, they begin to use some of the toys that represent life, but stay on the periphery, like army men or dinosaurs. As they get closer to expressing their feelings and emotions, they will use toys that are closer to representing themselves and their family, like the doll house with the wooden people. All along, I'm in the room with Andy, but I'm instructed to only play when he invites me and to let him have complete control. In other words, I don't make up any of the play, I only respond to what he tells me to do.

We are at the final stage where he moves from playing with the family and the house to playing directly with me. We use Nerf swords and guns. Samantha has told me that I need to express a lot of emotion so Andy knows that I understand what he is feeling.

Andy hands me a sword and tells me he is a ninja. I look scared. I get down on my knees so he's taller than me. He swings his sword at me, and I block him with my sword a few times. On the fourth swing he gets me in the side. I fall to the ground covering my wound with my hand and moan loudly. He waits for me to recover. I pick up my sword with my good hand, and he attacks again. This time he gets me on the other side. I fall again and grasp my other side moaning louder than before. He's anxiously waiting for me to pick up my sword again. I look at Samantha for reassurance that my acting is good enough. Although, it's not much of an act knowing that the pain Andy is inflicting on me is the same pain that I have inflicted on him during his young life. On one hand, I'm relieved that he is working through this anger and pain. On the other hand, it hurts to know the anger and pain he feels is my fault. It's easier at home when he's watching TV or playing video games to tell myself that he's fine, and he's too young to really have been hurt by me. It's easy to rationalize my mothering skills with a bottle of wine. But here, in this little play room, I'm staring at my son who is killing me with his sword while a professional watches us re-enact the emotional pain I put him through. Then I think about JB's comment that Andy has had his twitch since he was two years old. I think it would be less painful if Andy were using a real sword.

What kind of a monster was I that my two-year-old son would begin twitching?! I pick up my sword again. I want him to hurt me. I need him to hurt me because I can't stand what I've done, and I'm hoping that each time he wields his sword over me, he is able to erase the marks I left on him. With my sword in hand, I pretend I can barely move. He waits a moment, smiles and then charges at me. I can only partially block him this time and his sword goes right into my stomach. I fall forward to the ground. With my face on the floor, he can't see the tears that are forming. He has won the battle. I hope.

I'm thinking about this session as I walk into Jen's office and take my spot on the couch. The guilt I feel for being a terrible mom is tremendous. It weighs on me and pushes me further into the couch cushions.

"Andy's play therapy session with Samantha was yesterday."

She waits. I think. I feel. I breathe.

"How did it go?"

"It was really hard."

"How did you feel?"

"Horrible. Guilty. Like the worst mother in the world."

"What happened in Andy's therapy?"

"We had a sword fight. Every time he stabbed me I had to show that it hurt me, so he could see that I understood his pain."

"Wow. That's really brave of you to do."

I think of the word "brave." I can't connect that word to myself.

"It's more like sorry. I don't feel brave. I feel really terrible. What kind of mom puts their child through that much pain?"

"It's part of our human nature to hurt people we love without knowing. Relationships are messy. No one is perfect. We just have to do the best we can."

"My best wasn't good enough."

"So, what are you doing about it?"

"About not being good enough?"

"What are you doing to make things better?"

"Well, we're in play therapy."

"Yes. What else?"

"I'm in therapy to learn how to be a better mom."

"Yes. What else?"

"I went to treatment and I go to my twelve step meetings every week."

"Good. What else."

"I go to the DBT group every week."

"Yes. Anything else?"

I think for a moment.

"I don't think so."

"Do you hug him?"

"Yeah."

"Do you kiss him and hold him?"

"Yeah."

"Do you tuck him into bed?"

"Yeah."

"Do you feed him and clothe him and go on school field trips with him?"

"Yeah."

"You are a good mom, Jenny. You need to stop punishing yourself and give yourself some credit. You are doing everything you can right now, and that's all you can do. Can you change the past?"

I wish I could. I would give anything to change the past.

"No."

I think about a woman in our twelve step group. Every week she says the same quotes over and over. They were annoying at first, but they are making more sense as I get to know myself. She says, "You are right where you are supposed to be." I didn't get it until now. In DBT we talked about living in the present moment, but I had a hard time grasping the concept. Now it is coming together. I can't do anything about the past. All I can do is live in the moment I have right now, and that will help determine the future that I want. It doesn't help to feel guilty and depressed. That only makes the current situation worse.

As I take this all in, I begin to see a different picture of my situation. Instead of looking at my life and seeing a big pile of mud, I see a lump of clay. It doesn't look like anything right now, but I see the possibilities of what it could be. There are probably a million different things it could become, but I can't see the finished product. All I can see is the possibility of something. Some of my guilt starts to slide off my shoulders, and I begin to think that it's going to be okay. I just need to keep working toward the goal.

What is my goal? Terri, the DBT leader, asked us to put a picture or a phrase on our DBT workbooks that captures why we are in this group. It didn't take me long to think of a verse from a song I love by Sara Groves, *Generations will reap what I sow*. I think of how I was raised and how alcoholism runs in our family. And I think of how badly I don't want to pass it down to my kids. I looked up pictures on the internet and found one of a huge tree and another of a large, rusty chain that's broken. I print them out and put them on the front and back cover of my book. The tree stands for generations of my family; the good and the bad. The broken chain stands for the end of anger and rage in my family. I can see my kids growing up without alcoholism or anger in their lives, and I can see them as healthy people raising their own kids without addiction and anger. On the back cover of my book by the chains I write, "Breaking free." It surprises me how much these pictures motivate me to do the homework and to keep working on it when I want to quit.

"One of the things you need to learn in order to heal is radical acceptance."

I look at her with a blank stare.

179

"Radical acceptance means that no matter what the situation is, you need to accept that it isn't going to change. Sometimes there are people who just won't accept life as it is. They will do anything to deny it, but denying it doesn't make it go away. It just makes the situation harder for everyone else around them."

I think of my mom's denial and how it has affected my life. By insulating herself from pain and reality, she has forced the rest of us to deal with her issues. In my second or third week of therapy, Jen said that my emotional age was about thirteen and that usually we stop growing emotionally because of a traumatic event. My mom was only ten when her mother died and her emotional age seems about ten years old. For a moment it makes me feel sorry for my mom. Then I think of being forced to grow up living with my mom's denial and chaos, and my heart beats faster. My jaw clenches. My body is in fight mode, but my mind is telling me to calm down. If I can't calm down and accept my reality, then I am doing the same thing to my kids that my mom did to me.

"You can't move on to the future if you haven't accepted the past."

I'm trying to wrap my brain around this acceptance thing. My heart is on fire, moving between cold and hot air. I've already buried my childhood and cried about it. I don't know why I can't move on.

"What do you feel when you think about radical acceptance?"

"I feel mad."

"What do you feel mad about?"

"I feel mad about my life."

"What about your life."

"I feel like everything is on my shoulders. I have to forgive my parents for everything as well as work my butt off to become a good mom for my kids."

"Why is it hard to forgive your parents?"

"Because I feel like forgiving them is saying it's alright that they were bad parents."

"Do you think you could say, it's not alright, but I'm going to try to understand?"

My head drops and I stare at the floor.

"What do you know about your parents' childhoods?"

"I don't know a lot, but what I heard wasn't good. My grandpa sounded physically abusive when he was drunk, and he sounded drunk a lot of the time. I heard he threw my grandma down the stairs once. My grandma drank a lot too. She tied my dad and his siblings to the clothes line so they couldn't get out of the yard."

"What about your mom?"

"Her childhood wasn't good either. Her mom died of pneumonia in a hospital. Being ten years old, my mom wasn't able to go see her, and she never got to say goodbye. They packed up all their stuff and moved from the west coast to the east coast. My grandfather remarried six months later to a woman only 14 years older than my mom. My mom said her stepmother made her throw out all of her stuffed animals because she was too old for them. And my mom wasn't allowed to keep a picture of her real mother in her room. Her step mother sounded awful."

The more I talk, the more I see my parents as two broken children without anywhere to go.

"So, really, they were just kids emotionally, trying to raise their own kids."

"Yeah, I guess."

"Maybe you can do some journaling about your parents. Journaling seems to help you work through it."

"Ok."

"In your journaling about your parents, make sure you are writing about what you are feeling; not just events that happened, but what emotions do those events bring up inside of you."

My mind wanders to our DBT group and how we talked about secondary emotions. We keep talking about feelings and how we repress them or use a secondary feeling to hide the initial emotion. I stayed after group to ask Terri how to go from repressing feelings to feeling them. She said it was a process. I wanted her to just tell me where the button was so I could push it and find my feelings. Even though I don't want to feel them, I know I won't be healthy until I can, so I might as well try to do it and get it over with.

"In DBT this week we talked about secondary emotions, and I can't figure out how to know when it's secondary or when it's how I really feel. Whatever I feel seems real. Like when I'm angry. I feel angry, so how do I know if it's anger or if I'm really sad or depressed?"

"Let's use an example. When's the last time you felt angry?"

It doesn't take me long, because I feel like I'm always angry, but since we're talking about my parents, I think about the last time I talked to my mom.

"When my mom stopped by my house."

"What happened?"

"I was at home, and the dog started barking. I looked outside and my mom was at the door."

"Then what?"

"Well, sometimes I pretend I'm not home, but my car was in the driveway, and I thought she might have seen me, so I opened the door and let her in."

"Did you have a conversation with her?"

"We don't have conversations. She just talks. She starts the minute she enters the doorway and doesn't stop until she leaves."

183

"And how does that make you feel?"

"Most of the time I just ignore her and pretend like I'm listening."

"How does ignoring and pretending make you feel?"

I picture my mom in my entryway talking. I picture her with my siblings talking. I picture her with my kids talking. All I can see now is her talking and talking and talking and never listening. I can't remember an image of her where she isn't talking. I fight the urge to dismiss these thoughts, but that's exactly what Jen is asking me not to do. She wants me to quit ignoring these thoughts and start facing them. The more I let myself think about it the angrier I get.

"I feel angry."

"Why do you feel angry?"

"Because I don't like to be with her."

"Why don't you like to be with her?"

"Because she drains me of all my energy."

"What about her is draining your energy?"

I'm starting to feel the anger pulsing through my body as Jen digs for answers.

"She never stops! She just goes on and on and on about our dead relatives and some dead people who aren't even our relatives and what she's doing at church and all the problems going on at work and whatever other dumb thing is going on in her life. She spends 99 percent of her life doing genealogy, trying to figure out who some great, great, great grandmother is and where she's from, and then she hunts down their gravestones to record the dates of their birth and death. Who cares?! They're dead!"

Jen is quiet now letting my words float through the air and my heart beats fast with emotions. In the quietness I look at Jen and the concerned look on her face penetrates the anger I feel. It slowly cools off and as my heart slows, so do my thoughts, which make room for a new feeling to emerge. We sit quietly together, and my breathing slows more and my heart begins to ache. The pain runs up my chest and into my head. I feel itchy like I want to run or try to gather the anger back up, but it has evaporated, and I can't reach it. Jen breaks the silence.

"What do you feel right now?"

My lip starts to quiver, and my eyes fill with water. I turn away from her and swallow hard trying to hold the new feeling in check, but it has swelled too big to contain now, and I can't fight back this new emotion. I swallow hard again and try to speak.

"I feel hurt."

"Why?"

"Because I feel like she cares more about dead people than she does about me."

I hang my head and close my eyes. I want to crawl up on the couch and fall asleep. The pain keeps building and

185

rests on my heart like a big boulder. It's sharp and heavy, and I know now why I'm always angry, because anger is so much easier to feel than hurt. I can function with anger. It may not always look good, and I break a lot of things, but this pain is immobilizing. I feel like I was cast in wet cement and it's starting to harden, and I'll never be able to break out of the mold. Jen is listening and watching me. It feels like that's all I've ever wanted, to be seen. Being invisible hurts. I think back to my teen years when I found a way to be seen. I found that in sports people noticed me, and I played my heart out to be noticed. Sometimes the work paid off.

It's a perfect Minnesota summer day. I scrape my cleats across the hard dirt of the infield between second and third base. My friend, Carrie, is the pitcher, her sister is the catcher, and I'm at short stop. Carrie's dad coaches our summer softball team. My eyes are trained on the batter. I watch her practice swings and which way her feet are facing in the batter's box. I know from Carrie's pitching whether or not this girl will be able to swing fast enough to hit into left field. The batter doesn't have a good swing, but Carrie throws a changeup, and she hits it high left over third base, out of bounds. I could easily let this one go foul and it would be counted as a strike, but I can't let things go, and I'm sprinting with an intense focus on the ball. As I dive, my outstretched glove grabs the ball a foot off the ground and I slide to a stop keeping my glove in the air for the umpire to see. Carrie's dad is so excited, he's screaming and shouting and jumping up and down on the sideline. It wasn't a tournament game or anything important, but the catch was amazing, something right out of the movies. My heart swells up with pride, and I drink in every wonderful feeling this moment brings. Carrie's dad talks about it for weeks afterward. Every time it comes up I savor the attention and tuck some of it away for later when I'm lonely and thirsty for attention, and there's nothing else to drink.

As the memory fades and my mind wanders back to the couch I'm sitting on, the joy fades and the pain in my chest returns. Anger is so much easier to feel than disappointment and loneliness. Wanting something is dangerous, because wanting is on the verge of needing. And if I need something and can't get it, it's disappointing. No, it's more than that. Not getting my favorite toy for Christmas is disappointing. Not having a mom who could listen and know and understand me is physically painful. It's an ache that starts in my heart and reaches out to places inside of me I didn't know were there. It cuts off my air until it's hard to breathe. It's like trying to live on top of a mountain before adjusting to the altitude.

Letting go of the anger and letting myself feel the pain causes some of the hard pieces around my heart to crumble and the soft, bruised areas inside cringe at the fresh air seeping in. Mentally, I'm trying to grasp the crumbling pieces and put them back in place so my heart doesn't hurt so much, but the pieces turn to sand and run between my fingers. I'm slouched on the couch staring at the floor. Jen finally speaks.

"So, anger is probably a secondary emotion, then?"

"Yeah, probably."

"What do you think the primary emotion is?"

187

Several words come to mind: pain, hurt, loss. I wonder if any of these are emotions. Jen slowly pulls out my emotion worksheet and hands it to me. I look over the faces and descriptions. There is sad, exhausted and depressed, but none of those words describes the ache I feel. None of the emotions on the sheet hurt as much as I do, but I try to explain it anyway.

"It's sad, only more. Like when you see those starving children on the TV commercials and their eyes look dead. That's how I feel."

Session 17

I'm walking down the long hallway to Jen's office. I open the main door. Her office door is shut. I wonder if someone else is in there. I've never seen anyone else in the waiting room. I'm sure I'm not her only client, but I'm annoyed anyway. What a strange thought. I'm not three years old. I wonder if I'm more than thirteen yet, emotionally, I mean. I don't want to feel jealous. I sit down on the couch. A bunch of magazines are spread out on the coffee table. I look at the titles; *Parenting, Cooking Light, Women's Health, Family Fun, Good Housekeeping*. I pick up *Sports Illustrated*. I'm turning the pages, but I'm not really reading them. I look at my watch. My session is in two minutes. I wonder if they'll be done by then. I can hear muffled voices through the wall. I wonder if anyone has listened to me from this side of the wall. There was a mom and daughter here once in the waiting room after I was done. There are always people at the fancy place where Andy goes for his play therapy, but no one is ever here. I look at my watch. She's five minutes over. I'm worried. I might get five minutes less than my hour. I guess it would only be fair. She has let us go over an hour several times. I check her wall clock a lot, but I've never caught her checking it. It seems like she is really listening. She's always looking at me. I love that. And now she's looking at someone else. I hate that. I look back at the magazine. I still can't read it.

189

The door finally opens. A young woman walks out. They say good-bye. Jen turns to me. She is smiling. It's a big welcoming smile. Her whole face lights up when she smiles. I think Jen likes me better. I go in. The room is warm as usual. I sit on the couch and sink into my spot.

"How was your week?"

I have to think. I'm still wondering about that girl who was in here. She was in my spot on my couch. I need to think about something else. My time in here is sacred, and I'm not going to waste any of it thinking about that other girl. I wonder if Jen really likes me. Maybe she just likes everyone. What did she ask me? What did I do this week? How do I feel? Oh yes, I remember this week. It was a little crazy!

"It was a long week."

"How come?"

"I was trying to let myself feel stuff."

Somehow I'm learning to let go. I've heard the saying, "Let go and let God." I didn't get it. I still don't get it, but there has been a slight change in me. I'm able to let go of my anger sometimes. It's only for a moment or two, but that's just long enough to feel something. It sucks. It's crazy. Thirty years of emotions are buried inside me like lava in a volcano. All of our digging around is causing tremors, and I feel like I'm going to explode into pieces.

"What kinds of things are you feeling?"

190

"I don't know. It's really confusing. One minute I'm fine. Then I'm sad. Then I'm angry. Then I'm anxious. It's like somebody else takes over my body, and I can't control it."

"You've been burying your emotions for so long that they are finally coming to the surface. It will feel unnatural for a while because you're not used to feeling your emotions. You need to remember that they will come and then they will go, like a wave. When it feels uncomfortable just remember that they aren't going to stay forever."

I feel anxious right now, and what Jen says about the wave makes me think of my DBT group. We practiced being in the moment, just experiencing what we are feeling right now. Not tomorrow. Not yesterday. Just now. I think about how anxious I am. I practice a meditation exercise we did in group. I see my anxiety riding on a blue, white capped wave. I'm standing on the shore, and the wave comes in and washes over my feet. Then the wave goes back out, and my feet have buried themselves in the sand.

"How do you think you are handling the new emotions you're feeling?"

I'm scared, but I don't want to say that. I feel like my finger was plugging a hole in the dike. Now I'm starting to take my finger out and I'm scared the hole will lead to cracking, and soon all the emotions I dammed up will break through the dike and drown me. It happened on a small scale after my DBT group this past week and it scared me.

Group is over, and I'm sitting in my car. I need to get home. My kids are waiting, but I need some time to think.

191

We talked about secondary emotions, and I'm anxious to figure this out. My mind drifts to my parents. I've seen a picture of my mom as a little girl about ten years old. Her hair is white blond and long with big curls at the ends. Her eyes are iridescent blue, and it looks like she's staring at me. Her smile covers her whole face, so I figure it was taken before her mother died.

In high school my mom fell in love with a man named Richard. They planned to get married, but their parents made them wait until they were through college. While Richard was away at college my mom met my dad while he was stationed in D.C. They got married and moved back to my dad's home in Minnesota. My mom had never been in the Midwest, and he told her everyone in Minnesota spoke Norwegian. She bought some language record albums and began practicing. She practiced for two months before they arrived, and she didn't find out Minnesotans speak English until she asked the gas station attendant where the bathroom was in Norwegian. Their marriage started off on so many wrong notes it's amazing they made it twenty years before the divorce.

My mom stopped letting her mother-in-law babysit me when she realized her mother-in-law was an alcoholic and possible schizophrenic. Her father-in-law died of a heart attack before I was born. It's the first time I realize how lonely my mom must have been. With the violence my dad grew up with, I guess I should feel lucky that my dad was not always physically abusive.

I've always blamed my parents for my messed up childhood, but when I look at their own childhood, there's no way they could have done much better than they did. What did God expect would happen with those two messed

192

up children? Does he even care? If we're all broken and hurting each other, why did he design us to be in relationships?! I have so many questions now for God. I don't know where they came from. Just a little while ago I was teaching Bible study, and now I don't even believe God cares about me. I'm finally being honest, and I'm so mad I could put my fist through the windshield.

I pound on the steering wheel until my hands hurt. Tears stream down the side of my face. My heart aches. It's like a muscle I haven't used in years and now I keep working it, and I just want to quit because the pain is too much. I need a break. I'm trying to stay angry, but inside I'm melting. I'm grasping for the anger or anything that will cover the pain, but I can't reach it. It used to be automatic. I didn't even have to try. Anger was my response to anything and everything.

Tears are coming faster. Everything I've ever wanted from my parents was impossible from the start. Wishing they were happily married, wishing my mom would give up some church time to be with us, wishing my dad would set some rules because he loved us instead of screaming at us all the time, wishing my mom would be a mom instead of trying to be our friend, wishing she had been strong enough to hold me instead of looking to me for help. I rest my head on the steering wheel. My body shakes with my sobs. It surprises me how long it lasts. I guess I have fought it for so long that I've only ever let out a few tears here and there. Now it feels like the buckets of tears I've been storing all these years are pouring out like a river, and the current is so strong I can't help being swept away. The sobbing is so deep it doesn't make any sound and it feels like I've been dragged by the current into an *underwater cavern. I'm drowning in this cavern, but I don't care.*

Fifteen minutes go by. I try to lift my head off the steering wheel. I hurt on the outside now too, like I was in a rugby game. My eyes are swollen. I can hardly see. Tears are still running down my cheeks, but the shaking is gone. I remind myself of the wave we talked about in group. Emotions come and go. You are not your emotions. They too shall pass. I feel like I was washed up on shore after a ship wreck. I wipe the tears off my cheeks with my shirt sleeve. The pain is still there, but it's not so unbearable, and I think if I keep feeling things, maybe the pain will wash away and down the street and disappear into the gutters. I start the car and drive home. I know my kids are waiting for me to tuck them in.

I'm thinking now about Jen's question. How am I handling these new emotions?

"It's hard to deal with them instead of trying to get rid of them. My goal is to stay sober through all of my emotions."

I'm staring out the window. I turn my head to look at her. She is quiet. I'm getting more used to the silence. It feels good to just sit here and not talk.

"It can be hard, but it's good. Once you've allowed these new feelings and memories to come, it'll be easier to accept them. As you accept your past you'll be better able to heal and grow. The skills you're learning will help you deal with the emotions more effectively, and they won't feel so overwhelming. How are you doing with your anger?"

"I'm finding that a lot of my anger is covering pain."

"Pain from what?"

I don't want to talk about pain. I'd rather stick bamboo shoots under my fingernails.

"I think it's more from things that I didn't get than anything that actually happened."

"What kinds of things didn't you get?"

I look at the floor. I didn't have a lot of things like family vacations, cool clothes, money for lunch, but there's really only one thing that comes to mind that hurts.

"Attention."

"From your parents?"

"Actually, I got attention from my dad. It wasn't always good, but sometimes it was. He took us fishing, built bonfires so we could roast marshmallows and showed me how to read the stars."

I'm standing outside in the dark with my dad. He is pointing at the sky and showing me the Big Dipper. I feel excited as I see how the four stars make up the cup and the other three stars make up the handle. Then he asks me if I can see a little itty bitty star next to the second star in the handle. I look as close as I can. I tell him I think I see it. He tells me it's the Little Papoose, because it's a tiny star just off the bigger star in the handle, like an Indian baby wrapped in a papoose on his mom's back. He says if I can see the Papoose I have good eyes. I see a little tiny star twinkling on and off. I smile and my heart swells up so big it feels like it won't fit inside my chest anymore.

"It's my mom who I can't remember spending any time with. She was around some of the time. We spent a lot of time in the car or at church, but even though she was there, it was like she wasn't really there. It's sort of how I feel with my kids. I have to figure that out, because I don't want them to grow up that way."

"When you were drinking and depressed, you were very self-absorbed. You can't focus on someone else when you're focused on yourself. Your mom sounds like she has probably been in this kind of state since long before you were born. That will be up to her as to whether she does anything about it or not. The only thing you can control is you, right?"

"Yeah."

"You are doing something about your problem, and because of the work you're doing you can have a different relationship with your kids. The more you are willing to experience your emotions, the closer you will feel to your kids. This week I want you to continue to allow yourself to feel the emotions rising up inside you and keep journaling about your memories and experiences."

This feels like one of those catch-22 situations. In order to feel close to my kids, I have to allow myself to feel the pain of never feeling close to my mom. Some of these things don't make any sense, but I'm not willing to argue. My kids are more important to me than that.

Session 18

I'm pulling into the parking lot of Jen's office. I reach for my bag of notes which is underneath my Bible study book. I joined a Bible study at another church. Nancy decided to do a Bible study at her parents' church and asked me if I wanted to join her. I decided it would be nice to be at a church where no one knows me. We started the study a few weeks ago, and I like the other women in my group. I've done a lot of Bible studies over the years, but this one feels different. Instead of being the seasoned leader, I feel like I'm brand new. I guess in a way I am. I've never been so vulnerable and honest before. It makes everything feel like I'm doing it for the first time.

I get to Jen's office and walk in. I sit on the couch. Jen shuts her file drawer and grabs her tea. The warmth of her room makes it seem like I'm coming out of the cold air and being wrapped in a warm blanket.

"So, how are you?"

I'm trying to think before I blurt out some habitual phony phrase. I think about my week.

"I feel a little less anxious."

"Less anxious about anything in particular or just in general?"

"I don't feel as nervous and jumpy all the time. I can sit through my meetings better. I can go to the store without feeling self-conscious."

"Why do you think things are feeling better?"

I look out the window. It's a little overcast, but the sun looks like it wants to come out.

"I think I'm feeling less anxious because I'm starting to do some normal things again, like I am going to a Bible study with my friend. And I'm doing a little volunteering at the kids' school. It feels good to focus on something other than my recovery and therapy."

"I think the more you can balance out your activities, the less stress you'll feel in general."

There's that word "balance" again. It conjures up several other words like, boring, calculated, and impossible.

"So what are some ways you can continue to balance your recovery with your other life interests?"

I look at the floor.

"Maybe instead of just running I could start riding my bike and maybe read a book that isn't all about self-help and recovery."

"Those are great ideas. It was important for you to really focus on staying sober in the beginning, but now that it's been awhile, I think it's a good idea to start balancing out your life. You'll always be aware of your sobriety, but it's good for you to get involved in other activities."

"How are you feeling about your kids?"

"I've been trying really hard to give them my full attention when they're home. In DBT we talked about being in the moment, thinking about what's happening right now rather than what I need to do later or tomorrow."

I think about Johnny coming home after school yesterday. I wonder if there's such a thing as being too honest.

I'm washing dishes and the television is on. It's Dr. Phil drilling this couple on their parenting style. Johnny walks in the door. The kids are home from school. He begins to talk about his day. I'm still doing the dishes and my mind is preoccupied with Dr. Phil's accusations and this couple's confused reaction. I wonder if my parents aren't the only people who don't know how to be parents. Johnny is still talking. I can hear his voice but I don't know what he said. I know he's talking to me, so I respond with, "Uh huh." He asks me why I always say, "Uh huh." Now he has my attention because the question is intriguing to me. I reply to him without even thinking. I tell him that I say, "Uh huh" when I'm not really listening, so if he wants me to really listen he has to get my attention before he starts talking. After the words are out of my mouth I wonder if I should have come up with something that sounded better. I wonder if I hurt his feelings. I look at him. He looks at me. His eyebrows raise, and he asks me if I'm listening now. I try to block out the TV. I think about my new skill from DBT group of being in the moment. I have to tune everything else out to experience what is going on right now. I turn the water off in the sink and I look at him. "Yes, I'm listening now." He starts at the beginning and tells me about his day at school and the project they worked on. Then he pulls out

199

his poster and shows me what animal he chose to do for the nature project. I'm aware that I'm listening to him. Just him. I'm not doing the dishes. I'm not vacuuming. I'm not watching TV. I'm not on the computer. I'm just listening to Johnny talk. I ask him why he picked the cheetah. He tells me that cheetahs are the fastest animals in the jungle, and they can run 50 miles per hour. I tell him that's super-fast. We are communicating. He smiles. He knows I'm listening to him.

Dr. Phil's voice is still in the background screaming for my attention, and the dishes are still lying in the sink dirty. I fight my need to go finish them. I grab the remote control and turn off the TV. I ask Andy and Jenna to come to the kitchen. We all sit down at the table and I start asking everyone questions about school. Their eyes light up and they are suddenly like water pitchers pouring out everything that happened during their day. I try to get them to talk one at a time, but they are all talking at once, and none of them seem to care that they are talking over each other. This is what I've been missing? It's hard to believe that dirty dishes and Dr. Phil have been keeping me from this connecting time with my kids.

"It's hard to stop what I'm doing to listen to them, but I'm doing it, and it's really cool."

Jen smiles. I smile back. I don't look at the floor this time. I keep looking at her. I feel embarrassed, but I feel good. I know I did something right. It seems so little and so big at the same time. I guess I need to remember not to compare myself to other people. Just because that might be easy for other moms doesn't mean it was easy for me.

"Do you remember your report from the ADD clinic? You struggle with OCD. So once you are focused on a task you have a hard time switching gears to focus on something else."

I forgot about that. It explains a lot. I've never thought of myself as OCD because I don't wash my hands a thousand times a day or check the locks on my doors, but I do get very focused on things. Sometimes I'm so focused that I get really angry when I'm forced to stop working on something.

"So, it's really incredible that you were able to overcome that to sit still and listen to your kids!"

Maybe it's not such a little thing.

"I think you should keep practicing giving your attention to your kids when they're at home. That would be a really great exercise for you. You'll probably have to use a lot of your DBT skills."

"Yeah, I think that's a good idea."

I reach for my notebook in my bag. I take out a pen and try to find the last page I took notes on. I can't find it, so I make a new page. I wonder how often I can't find the notes I'm taking. Probably a lot. I think it helps just to be writing them down even if I can't find them again. I write down, "Give my full attention to my kids every time they talk to me." That's a big goal, but I'm determined to do it.

"It's really good that you are getting involved in things other than recovery, but you need to make sure you don't overdo it. Take your time and check your calendar when you make commitments."

"Actually, Nancy and I were talking about that, and I decided one way I can keep from overcommitting is to run ideas by her before I say yes to anything."

"That's a great idea. Have you been carrying your calendar around?"

"Some of the time."

I was really frustrated about my calendar for a while because I'd forget it or lose it. Then I remembered how long it took to remember to hang up my car keys. I used to lose my keys a few times a week. Then I put up a key holder by the garage door. It took about six months for it to become a habit to hang up my keys as soon as I walked in the door. It will probably take more than a few weeks to remember to bring my calendar with me everywhere.

"You've probably heard it takes 21 days to form a habit. So, if you can put your calendar somewhere that you'll remember it for 21 days, you will reduce your vulnerability to your old chaotic lifestyle. It's like running reduces your vulnerability to depression. How has your running been going?"

"That's getting better. It's still hard to stop and turn around to stay at 35 minutes instead of running the whole five mile loop, but maybe that is some OCD too and not just my addictive personality forcing me to do more."

"How is that?"

"I was wondering why I feel such a need to run my five mile loop, and I realized that running a full circle makes me feel better than running half a mile down a road and turning around and coming back. There's no ... symmetry or something."

"Maybe you could find a full circle that is only 35 minutes long."

I think about some of the other roads around my house that might work, but I don't like any of them. They are all neighborhood roads. I like getting out of our neighborhood. We live right across the street from a lot of farmland. When I run by the fields I feel like I'm in the country, and I love it.

There was an old farm house I used to run by. The paint was chipping off, and the windows were broken. The grass was overgrown and the barn looked like it was going to fall over. The fading name on the mailbox made me wonder about the people who lived there. One day as I was running by I noticed the house was gone. There was a large area of dirt where the house once stood. Trees surrounded the empty space like people dressed in black gathered around a burial site. The branches swayed with the breeze never looking away from the empty space. The mailbox continued to stand at the end of the driveway for the rest of the summer. I felt sad every time I ran by the empty lot. It reminded me that every time I get used to something or someone they disappear. It feels like the world is a rug, and people keep pulling it out from underneath me. I never know where to stand.

"No, I don't want to run anywhere else. My route is comfortable."

"Well, since your running is a form of meditation for you, it's good that it's comfortable."

"I'm just getting tired of all the changes. It's exhausting. I need something to stay the same."

"Recovery is definitely a time of change. You could probably use some more meditative exercises when you feel a lot of stress. Can you think of some other things you can do or places you can go that make you feel calm when your stress level is high?"

"I thought my Bible study was going to be a comfortable place, but it's not turning out to be that way."

"Why is that?"

"Now that I've been more honest with myself I'm finding that I'm really angry with God."

I'm waiting for lightning to strike through the window and hit me on the couch. Jen must sense my fear.

"Do you know that it's all right to be mad at God?"

"Well, I've heard that, but it still feels wrong to be angry at him."

"Do you think God already knows you are mad at him?"

"Yeah."

"So, if he already knows, then there's no reason to pretend, right?"

"Yeah, but it's like maybe he'd understand if I knew I wasn't supposed to be mad at him even though I am."

"I think God wants you to be honest with him, not for his sake, but for your own sake."

The idea about being mad at God is floating around in my head, bouncing off the walls like a pinball machine. I'm not sure where the ball is going exactly, but like my anger, every time the ball gets close to going out of play, I push the flippers wildly to keep the ball moving.

"What are you angry about?"

I was hoping we wouldn't get to this. I want to sweep it under the rug, but there are no more rugs. I can sit still, but there's nowhere to hide. I take a deep breath. I can't open my mouth. I thought it would be easier to talk about the second time, but it's not. Maybe it never will be.

"I'm angry that God let me... be raped."

"That's good."

I'm so confused. That was hard to say out loud. I wasn't expecting her to be happy about it.

"What about your rape is causing you to be angry at God?"

Her question brings me back to a conversation I had with a friend. The only people who knew about my rape were JB, Nancy, Ann and Jen. But I have another friend who was sexually abused, so I felt like I could trust her. I knew she would understand. It was hard to talk about, but it seems like talking about hard things helps me get them out of my head and into the open where I can deal with them.

I'm sitting on a wooden chair in Lori's apartment. I hesitate to talk. Lori is a good listener like Jen. She asks me what's bothering me. I tell her that I'm stuck. I'm having trouble with counseling because God is supposed to be my rescuer in all this mess, but now I'm mad at him and don't trust him, so I don't know what I'm supposed to do. She asks why I'm mad at God. I breathe deep. I look at the floor and the wall. I look everywhere but into her eyes. I start to talk, but I can't get out any coherent words. She is patient and quiet. She tells me it's ok. I take another huge breath and find a small spot on the floor to focus my attention. Then I tell her that I can't understand why God allowed me to be raped. I'm still staring at the spot on the floor, but it's getting blurry. I look up at her for a moment because I need to find some comfort in her eyes. I find it and look back to the floor. She tells me that God didn't just let it happen to me. He loves me very much, so much that he was there with me through all of it.

My jaw tightens. My eyebrows crease. He was with me. I stand up and thank her for dinner. I need to get out of here now! I need to run. I open the door. She says goodnight. I get in the car. I start it and back down the driveway fast. It's a dirt road, and my tires spew rocks everywhere as I step hard on the gas. What is that supposed to mean?! He was there with me through it all! I know she was trying to say something comforting, but it infuriates me. He was there watching me go through all that physical and emotional pain?! How is that supposed to be comforting?! At least when I imagined God was too

206

busy to help me, I could fathom that I wasn't important enough for him to take the time to help me, that there were bigger things going on in the world than me being raped. Besides, I got myself into that bad situation. Now I'm going to have to pay the consequences of being there and being drunk. What did I expect was going to happen?! He's not just going to rescue me from every situation I get myself in. But how could God just sit in that room and watch that boy hurt me?! Tears are streaming down my face. I can't see the road very well. I should slow down, but I don't. What kind of God watches his children being abused and molested and tortured and killed?! What possible reason could he have to let these kinds of things happen?!?! I race down the road wiping tears from my eyes. I'm so mad I want to run over someone. I want someone to run over me. I just want something to happen! This can't be right!

My mind wanders back into Jen's office. I'm mad, and I can't figure this out.

"How could God let it happen? How can he stand by while terrible things happen to his children and he has all the power in the universe and he doesn't use it to save us! How can that be okay? I can't follow a God like that!"

Jen's face saddens. She feels my pain, and it touches me. We are both quiet. I feel guilty that I made her sad, but I also feel angry. I want to close myself off from the world, but her reaction keeps me from closing off completely. The way she looks inside me keeps me from hardening every part of my heart. There's a little tiny space that she is keeping warm and soft. It hurts to leave that part of my heart uncovered. I want to shut down everything, be done with this therapy and my groups and just let myself be angry and drink all this pain away, but Jen's compassion touches me and I can't shut it out. After a long silence she finally speaks softly.

"That is a question that everyone has to face someday."

This is not the answer I was looking for. Somehow I know there is no answer, but I still want one. I don't see how I can move on until I get an answer. If I can't trust God, I can't just go along with life as usual.

I've heard that we wouldn't be able to make choices if we weren't allowed to do bad things and if we do bad things, then other people suffer. I also heard that God's ways are higher than our ways. That's not good enough anymore. The one answer I heard that did make sense, was that God doesn't actually make bad things happen to us in order to punish us, but he does allow things to happen to us for a reason. That made sense in some situations, but what possible reason could he have to allow someone to rape another person?

And what kind of father is able to watch his child go through so much pain, when he is strong enough to stop it?! There is no way I could sit and watch my child go through something like that. And he is supposed to be my father! I know his ways are higher than mine, but I can't accept that his higher ways mean I get raped!

"God is big enough to handle our questions and he wants us to ask those questions. He knows we aren't going to grow unless we are willing to be honest."

Jen is losing me. I get lost easily when I'm angry. I have a hard time seeing anything clearly. I have an intense desire to run. I want to run until my body collapses. I feel rage and pain, and I don't want to feel anything anymore!

I look past Jen to the wall. Rage is boiling inside of me. I don't want her to see it. I'm not mad at her. She is keeping me from drowning in this mess. I need to get out of here. I look at the clock. Our time is just about up. I notice a painting on the wall. It's abstract and colorful. It looks kind of messy, but there's something about it that makes it kind of beautiful. I have an urge to put my fist through it.

Session 19

I'm in church and my friend is on stage singing. I love her voice. Her brother is dying of cancer. Her dad already died of cancer and her mother is in remission. I know she is hurting. I wonder how she is able to sing with all the pain in her life. The words she is singing blow me away. "I'll praise you for you are holy, Lord, and I'll lift my hands, but you are worthy of so much more." I am stunned. A sea of emotion is rising in my chest. She is sitting on a stool staring up at the ceiling, and singing as if no one else is here. I can't take my eyes off her. Her voice draws my emotions to the surface. Part of me wants to cry. Another part of me is wrestling my emotions back into their place, locked tightly inside my heart. It makes me want to get up and run out of church, but I can't walk out while my friend is singing. I clench my teeth and fists. I don't want to feel anything but anger.

I close my eyes and wonder. I wonder about trust, and God, and people, and sorrow. I'm tired of vacillating between anger and sorrow. I wonder if I'll ever be happy again. I don't know what to think about God. I want to walk away and pretend I never believed in him. But I've seen him do things! I've seen things I can't explain. So, does he love to torture us? I feel like an ant under the magnifying glass of a little mischievous boy. Go ahead and burn me! It can't hurt any worse than I already feel.

I walk across the parking lot to Jen's office. I'm thinking about my friend, Amy. I asked her how she sang that song at church when so many things are happening in her life. She said she gets angry at God, but she still trusts him. I don't get it. She must know something I don't.

I walk into the office. I don't know what we're going to talk about today. I don't remember if I was supposed to work on something or not. I feel like a zombie. I'm really trying to be less stubborn and do what Jen or Nancy or Ann suggests, but it still feels very awkward. It feels like putting my shoes on the wrong feet. It's hard to go against my gut feeling and trust someone else, but I've already proven I can't trust myself. I sit on Jen's couch and stare at the wall. Jen sits in her chair. I wonder how she listens to crazy stories and frustrating people all day long and still smiles. I take a deep breath.

"How are you today?"

"I'm tired."

"Are you getting enough sleep?"

"Probably."

"Are you running?"

"Yeah."

"Are you eating well?"

"Sort of."

I really never eat well. I don't eat horribly, but I don't go out of my way to eat healthy. I don't like to spend that much time thinking about food. I get hungry. I go to the kitchen. I make the quickest thing I can find. It's usually a peanut butter sandwich. I have my stash of Hershey bars in a file drawer so my family doesn't eat them all, and there is always plenty of sugar cereal in the cupboard.

"What did you do this week?"

I hate trying to remember my whole week. I have a hard time remembering yesterday. JB thinks I learned how to forget things as a child, so I didn't have to think about my life. It makes sense to me. I suppose that's why people with really traumatizing experiences often don't remember much of their childhood.

"How are you doing with your kids?"

I think about my visit to their elementary school.

I've parked in the school parking lot. I have to drop off Jenna's lunch. She forgot it on the kitchen table when she ran out to catch the bus this morning. Every time I go to the school it reminds me that I failed my kids. I check in at the office and head to the third grade hallway and look for the lockers marked with American flags. Each class has their own picture so the kids can find their lockers easier. I'm thankful, because it helps me a lot. I find her locker, open it up and place her lunch on the top shelf. I wonder if she'll see it. I don't want her to go without lunch today, and I don't want her to worry in class about her lunch. Maybe I could sneak down to her class to let her teacher know. I walk to the third grade classrooms. There are some kids in the reading area outside of the class. Jenna is sitting on the floor next to a volunteer mom. Jenna is reading a book as the mom listens. Jenna is stuck on a word. The mom starts sounding out the word with her. Jenna follows along, "Wednnnnesday, Wednesday!" The mom smiles big and nods her head acknowledging her progress. Jenna smiles. She looks proud of herself.

I stand still for a moment as the weight of my failure holds me captive to this spot. I think back to my homeschooling methods. Jenna has a hard time sitting still, so when we're done going over the lessons, she has to keep working until she's done with her homework. One day that took hours. She was particularly fidgety. Andy had long since finished all his work so I let him go play. I sat next to Jenna and told her I would work next to her so she could focus better. Thirty seconds later I got up to do some things. I realized while doing the dishes that I needed to go back and sit with Jenna. She was off track again. I sat by her and tried to get some work done. I couldn't focus, so I got up and put some of the science supplies away. Jenna became distracted again, so I sat down next to her. I decided to help her so she could be done and I wouldn't have to sit here all day going crazy. I could not get her to think about the homework, so I finally got up, grabbed a winter scarf and tied her to the chair. I kept her there until I realized as I was pacing around the house, that I couldn't sit there any longer than she could! Who ties their kid to a chair?! Not those homeschool moms I see at the conventions with their home-made denim jumpers and ponytails cascading down their back. I'm sure they had all twelve of their kids sitting around the table quietly doing their lessons and finishing homework two grades ahead of their age. Who did I think I was that I could homeschool my kids?!

213

I can't believe I've put Jenna in this situation where she's behind the other kids in her class. I'm jealous that this mom is connecting with my daughter like it's the easiest thing in the world to sit there and sound out the words together. I need to leave before Jenna sees me. I will myself to turn and walk away. I stare at the pavement as I walk to my car. I want to escape, but there's nowhere to go. I want to do something, but I realize I am doing all I can. I need to accept that I'm doing all I can.

"I still feel bad about what I've done to my kids."

I look at the floor. I hate admitting my terrible parenting. It's embarrassing. I deserve it though. Jen is quiet.

"I know I can't do anything about the past. I know I have to keep looking ahead and working on myself. It's just hard to watch them have to go through hard things because of me. They didn't do anything to deserve what I've done to them."

Jen is quiet for a moment before she responds.

"Neither did you."

I sit still as her words penetrate my mind. They are sinking in slowly like rainwater draining into the soil. I replay them; I didn't do anything to deserve what I got. Didn't I? Why have I never thought of that? I don't feel undeserving. I feel guilty, like I have deserved every bad thing that has ever happened to me.

"You are so hard on yourself. You expect yourself to be the perfect parent without having anyone to model it for you. Everyone else in the world follows human nature and repeats the patterns they grew up with, but you think you're different; that you should magically be able to overcome your childhood and be the perfect parent. Like we talked about, adult children of alcoholics believe that everyone is doing life the right way, and they are doing it wrong. They also believe they should be doing everything different because they learned how terrible it is to parent poorly. That's just not how human behavior works. We repeat the patterns of our parents, because that's what we know."

I begin to think of the similarities between myself and my parents. I've seen the similarities, but I've dismissed them from my mind as quickly as they came, because I can't stand the thought of resembling my parents. I have a bad temper like my dad. I spent a lot of my time at church looking for affirmation like my mom. I'm a perfectionist like my dad. I'm really stubborn like both of my parents. I hear myself saying the same things to my kids that they said to me. I've tried so hard to not be like them, and I see them in myself all the time.

"You need to stop dwelling on what you've done wrong, and start looking at what you're doing right. Use some of the skills you've learned to focus on what you can do rather than what you can't do."

"Ok."

"Are you doing everything you can to make life better for you and your kids?"

I think about all my recovery stuff; inpatient treatment, outpatient treatment, twelve step meetings, therapy, DBT group, practicing my skills to have better behavior. I still want to be better than I am, but I can't think of anything more that I could do to make things better.

"I guess so."

"So you are doing everything possible to make your life and your family's lives better?"

"I guess so."

"You should be proud of yourself for working this hard to make all these changes. Not many people are willing to change. Can you say that you are doing a good job?"

I look at the ceiling. I hate this.

"I'm doing a good job."

Saying it out loud actually makes me feel like I really am doing a good job. I think I would have quit awhile back without the constant encouragement I get from my friends. They celebrate my smallest little achievements even though I think they're not big enough to really celebrate. It feels good to hear them tell me how I'm doing and remind me how far I've come. I'm always looking at what I haven't accomplished yet. I'm beginning to feel the importance of being proud of the work I have done already no matter how small it might seem. It's another habit I need to learn that feels uncomfortable and awkward right now.

Everything feels awkward now, especially talking to JB. I think I'm beginning to earn his trust back a little bit. In the first few weeks after I got out of treatment no one let me drive at all. My friends gave me rides to my meetings and JB did all the driving after he got home from work. When I finally started driving he would ask where I was going and how long I would be gone and if I was going with anyone. It drove me crazy, but I understood why he was paranoid. I'd been drinking for three years, and he didn't know it. We talked about it a little one night. I thought he didn't know anything, but he did know something was up. He knew I was distant and preoccupied, and I avoided him a lot. He broke down when he said he thought I was having an affair. I was a little stunned at first, but the more I thought about what my alcoholism must have looked like from his perspective, the more sense it made. In some ways, I was having an affair with alcohol. I've heard a lot of alcoholics and addicts explain their relationship to a drug as an affair. It starts out innocently, but soon you're hooked and you wonder how you got there, and then the drug is all you want and all you need. Now I have to repair the damage I've caused and it won't happen overnight. There is no one big thing I can do to resolve my problems. I just have to be patient as I work through my program, but I have no patience. I want to fix everything right now. I can say I'm sorry all I want, but I know he won't trust me just because I said, I'm sorry. I need to keep making good decisions every day. It's one of the reasons I don't want to drink and mess things up again. I don't know how many times I can mess up and still earn his trust back.

"Have you been communicating with JB?"

"More than I used to."

"I think it's really important that you keep sharing with him how you feel everyday."

217

"Ok."

"Are you sharing something with him once a day?"

"Not every day."

"Is it starting to feel natural at all?"

"Not really."

JB and I are sitting on the couch watching TV. I realize I haven't told him how I feel today. I don't want to do it tonight. But I want to do this therapy stuff. I need to say something. It's not like we never talk to each other. We have three kids. We have to talk. But we don't talk about feelings. I bet most guys would be happy to never talk about feelings. I need to do this. What do I feel? I feel tired. That's not really a feeling word. I feel vulnerable. I don't want to tell him that. Way too scary. Maybe I can say I'm grouchy. That's a little less emotional. I look at him watching TV. I start talking. "You know how I'm supposed to tell you how I feel?" "Yes," he responds. "I feel grouchy." He wrinkles his eyebrows and begins to open his mouth. I cut him off. "You don't have to say anything. I just need to tell you." He responds, "Ok." We both go back to watching TV.

"Keep practicing with him."

I can't imagine it ever feeling natural to share my feelings with anyone.

"Are you doing anything fun just for yourself?"

"Like what?"

"Like the list you made of fun things to do."

I think about my list. Most of the stuff on there was bogus. I just wanted to get ten things on the page so I could be done with it.

"I mowed the grass this week."

"Does that count as a fun thing?"

"I really like mowing the lawn. It's very meditative."

"Are you doing anything besides chores?"

I think about the photo albums I laid out on my table to take to my friend's cabin.

"Some of my friends and I are going to a cabin for the weekend to scrapbook."

"That's sounds like fun!"

I think of the last time I worked on my scrapbook. It took me an hour to do one page. At this rate it would take me 240 years to scrap them all.

"I'm trying to be less of a perfectionist. It makes it difficult to have fun. I get frustrated."

"I'm glad you're noticing your perfectionism as a problem. Besides being a perfectionist, your OCD is probably causing you some trouble too."

Sometimes it's not that Jen says something brilliant, it's that we've laid out so many different pieces to the puzzle

219

that I'm starting to be able to find the corner pieces and then the edge pieces and when pieces fit together I can see a little bit more of the big picture. My OCD or perfectionism or whatever is going on is shedding some light on things I do that cause problems, like my writing.

I'm in my office at home in front of the computer. I'm writing a skit for the church Christmas program. I'm near the end and I haven't quite figured out how to resolve the problem I created between the characters. I start rereading from the beginning. I think I know where this is going. I need to go back and rewrite one of my character's lines. I need her to realize something earlier in the story so when I end the story, she will have come full circle. That's it! I scramble to find her lines. I'm deleting and rewriting. My thoughts are racing through my fingers onto the computer keyboard. "MOM! I'm ready!" Andy is calling to me from upstairs. He is ready to get tucked in. "I'll be up in a minute!" I stare at the screen. I reread what I just wrote. I'm writing again. I finish the scene and move to the next. I read through her lines. I make a couple of changes so it's now congruent with the first scene changes. I'm reading through the last scene. Ideas are coming. They are in my head, beginning to surface. I know the resolution is close. I continue to read and type and read and type. I'm almost there. Two or three more lines to go. "MOM!" Andy is yelling at me again. I'm so irritated I want to throw my computer across the room. Instead I yell, "JUST A MINUTE!!!"

I lost my thoughts. I only have a few more lines. All the thoughts were right at the tip of my tongue and now I can't remember what they were. AHHHH! I breathe in deep. I go back to the beginning of the scene. I start reading. As I read, the frustration starts to fade. The thoughts are coming again. I continue reading and I know what has to happen now. I begin to type. I delete. Not the right wording. I type again. Closer, but not perfect. I'm thinking. I'm tapping my foot and my mind is going 100 miles an hour. It's so close. I start typing again and it's coming together. Three more words. Done! It's done. I need to read it through to make sure it all works together. I look at the clock. Crap. It's been an hour since I told Andy I would be up. I walk upstairs and peak into his room. He's sound asleep. All the satisfaction I feel about my skit crumbles into a heap on the floor. I kneel beside Andy's bed and pull the covers up to his chin. I lean over and kiss his cheek. I wonder what he thought about while he was waiting for me. I wonder how many times I've done this and if his heart still breaks when I don't come up or if he's gotten to the point like I did as a kid where I just didn't have any more expectations.

My head feels like a lead weight as I add another check mark to my list of bad parenting skills. There are so many bad habits I need to change, and it's a constant struggle to remember the new skills I'm learning and be aware of when I need to use them. It's exhausting. I thought being an athlete was hard work. In basketball our coach made us run sprints after we lost one game in particular. We ran until someone threw up.

The physical challenges I've been through in high school and college sports are nothing compared to the mental exhaustion I've been through in recovery and therapy. Some days I can't stay awake, and I take a nap before the kids get home from school. I know I couldn't do this for any other reason than my kids.

221

"It seems like I don't have much time for fun. I've been trying to do fewer things to keep my schedule more open."

"Good. Everyone needs some margin. But you also need to make room for self-care. There will always be dozens of things vying for your attention. You need to schedule the things that are important first and then if there's room at the end of the day, you can deal with some things that are not as important. But you need to prioritize you time."

That's a good reminder. I've seen different prioritizing strategies for planners and calendars. I keep trying different organizing ideas, but they never work, because I usually don't remember by the next day that I was working on something. It gets very frustrating when I find remnants around the house of things I've started and forgotten about.

"So, let's make a priority list."

"Ok."

I get out some paper and my pen and write, "Priority List" at the top.

"What are the priorities in your life?"

"My kids."

"Good. What else?"

"My husband."

"Good."

"Friends."

"What else?"

"My recovery meetings."

"Good. What else?"

"Running."

"Anything else?"

"I think that's about it."

"How many of these priorities are on your calendar?"

"Not many."

"Then they really aren't a priority to you. You might think and say they are your priority, but the things you spend time on are the things you give value to. They are your priorities."

I ponder this thought as I stare at my calendar. There is a lot written down, but not much about my family. I have Bible study, twelve step meetings, coffee with a friend, and a dental appointment. Before I went to treatment, my kids always came last on my calendar. I spent time with them while I homeschooled them, but that was a different kind of time. They had to sit and listen to me. I wonder if I should actually make a date and time to sit and listen to my kids. It reminds me of something that happened this week.

I'm folding laundry. Andy and Jenna are at the table doing homework. I'm thinking about something Ann said today on the phone. It was just a trivial thing to her, but it stuck with me. She told me she's going to buy Star Wars plates and napkins for her son's birthday along with some green balloons because that's her son's favorite color. I wonder what Jenna's favorite color is. Why don't I know that? I wonder if all good parents know their kid's favorite color. I ask Jenna what her favorite color is. She tells me it's sometimes blue and sometimes purple. I ask Andy. He tells me silver. Wow, weird. I ask him why. He says because no one else likes silver. What an interesting answer. I realize this is a window into his personality. He's always been drawn to the kids that no one else likes, and he doesn't mind being different. He's got a lot of leadership qualities. I hope he will be able to see those qualities someday. I'm worried I've damaged his self-confidence.

I stop folding laundry and sit at the table with them. I look at Andy's homework. I ask him what he's doing. He says math. I look at his math book. There are a lot of fractions all over the page. I ask him if he knows how to do these. He says yes. I guess he doesn't need my help. I look at Jenna's homework. She's working on a list of spelling words. She has to come up with a sentence for every word. I ask her if she wants help. She says yes. She is excited. So am I. The first word is book. She looks at the word. Then she says, "Mrs. Sheraton helped me read the book." She smiles wide. I force myself to smile back as I imagine Mrs. Sheraton sitting with Jenna at school helping her learn to read. I feel like someone punched me in the stomach. She moves onto the next word. I help, but I don't know what I'm saying. I'm still wishing I had been Mrs. Sheraton today.

"I sat down with my kids this week and asked them questions."

"That's great. How did it go?"

"I'm usually trying to multi-task, so I'm always doing something else when they are talking to me, but I sat down with them at the table while they were doing homework and tried to focus just on what they were doing. It took some conscious thought to stay in my chair and ask questions and listen to their responses. But I felt we broke down some of the barriers between us."

"That is great. That's exactly what we're talking about when we talk about priorities. Putting your chores or other projects aside and giving someone your whole attention. It makes people feel important. If you never got that when you were a child, it is probably a foreign concept to you, so you'll have to keep consciously practicing it."

I think about being a kid, and I try to remember having someone's undivided attention. I got it from my dad sometimes when he was drunk. It seemed like undivided attention when he lectured us on space aliens or survival skills, but it also seemed like it didn't matter who he was talking to. We probably could have put our stuffed animals at the kitchen table with him, and they would have received the same undivided attention. It wasn't a question and answer session, just a lecture. I don't remember my mom ever sitting down and talking to me. I don't remember her ever sitting down. And if she was talking, there were no questions, just her own monologue.

My successful conversation with my kids and the lack of conversation I had with my parents is helping me understand how to get past some of the hurdles in my relationships. It's also beginning to explain why I'm having trouble figuring out intimacy in relationships. Intimacy must be more than a physical feeling. It must be the connection made by listening and understanding another person. And not just understanding, but somehow giving value to the way the other person thinks and feels and experiences life. If I can practice this with my kids, maybe I can start practicing this with other people in my life, and I won't feel like I live on an island.

Session 20

I'm sitting in my car in the parking lot of Jen's office. It's been two weeks. I don't like waiting that long. I know I have to start finding answers for myself. I have to stop depending on her so much even though I feel like I just started. I'm supposed to be using the skills I'm learning in DBT. Things like, meditating. I still hate meditating, but it is getting easier. I hate to admit it, but I think it actually helps. When I meditate in my DBT group my mind doesn't seem to race as fast anymore.

I look at the time. I need to go into my session. I grab my bag and walk to Jen's office. There is new carpeting and tile in the hallway. It looks like a whole new building. I go inside her office and everything is the same. I guess it could be updated in here too, but I don't really want it to change. I like it the way it is. I walk in and sit on the couch. The room is not very big. The small couch and end table almost cover the width of the office. There's just enough room for her desk, office chair, arm chair and book shelf. I guess the surroundings don't matter when everything else is right.

"How are you today?"

"I'm good."

"What did you work on the last couple of weeks?"

227

I quickly think of something non-emotional.

"I kept my running to 35 minutes. It's getting easier."

"Good. Why do you think it's getting easier?"

"I think it's easier because I'm not as worried about how fast I'm going. I started using our observation skills from DBT group."

"How are you doing that?"

"I look at the things I'm running by, like the barn and the houses and the corn fields. I'm trying to pay attention to them like I'm trying to pay attention to my kids."

"So you're being mindful by observing."

"Yeah."

"How do you think that makes a difference while you're running?"

"At first it was hard to think about anything but running and my time and distance. Then I tried running without my watch on so I couldn't time myself. That was really hard, but it forced me to look at the things around me. I didn't go again without my watch because my anxiety gets too high, but I knew I was supposed to focus on observing and looking around so I did, and the more I looked at things, the more relaxed I felt."

I smile as I think about my last run.

I'm running down the asphalt path alongside the tar road. The first half-mile is always the hardest, but I'm not timing myself today. I'm just going to enjoy the scenery. There are ball fields on the other side of the road. On one field a game has started. On another field a father and son are practicing batting. I'm running downhill past a mail box. The mail box is almost exactly a half-mile from my house. It's one of the spots I usually check my watch to see if I'm running at a good pace. I resist the urge to look at my watch.

I look back to the fields to get my mind off the watch. Beyond the baseball fields is a big sand pit. At the corner I turn onto the dirt road. This is my one mile marker. I start to look down at my watch, but quickly remember not to look. I look instead down the long stretch of road in front of me. It's my favorite part of my run because it's a dirt road and there's not much traffic. Corn is growing on either side of me, and it's getting too high to see over. Halfway up the road are two huge oak trees standing together in the corn field. The tips of their branches form a perfect circle in the sky. I pass them on my way up a hill. On my old five-mile run, I would go all the way down this road and around the corner, but since I'm only running 35 minutes I turn around at the top of the hill. If I'm running at a good pace, this is where I would hit 17 ½ minutes, which is half of my 35 minute run. I'm dying to know if I'm really at the halfway mark or if I'm a half a minute slower or faster. I resist the urge to look.

I turn around and begin running downhill. The running shoes I wear make distinct footprints. I see some other footprints and look at their stride to see if it's longer or shorter than mine. I think they are actually my own footprints from yesterday. I look up to see if there are any cars coming. I should be all the way over to the side of the road so I don't get hit, but I like running on the packed down area where the tires of the cars have worn a nice smooth path. I'm getting closer to the oak trees. I see a couple of large birds sitting on the branches. I don't think anything of it until I'm about 20 yards away. That's when I see the white head. They're eagles! The first one jumps off his perch and spreads his wings. It takes my breath away. The wingspan reaches almost all the way across the road. The other eagle follows, and I can't take my eyes off them. I watch them until they are small dots on the horizon, and then they disappear.

It's then that I realize I've stopped running. I'm standing still, completely unaware of my breathing or the distance I'm losing by this interruption or the fact that I've ruined my chance to feel my runner's high. Amazingly, I don't feel angry or frustrated, just peaceful as I continue to stare at the horizon.

"I think this is a great step for you. Learning how to observe and not judge yourself will greatly reduce your anxiety, and I think it will help you start connecting better in your relationships."

I think about how observing relates to my relationships. Andy comes to mind. In his play therapy sessions his therapist is basically asking me to observe what and how he plays. The whole hour I'm supposed to be watching him and reacting to him the way I think he wants me to react. He leads and I follow. It's all about him and what he wants to do with our play time. It's hard to focus my attention on him the whole hour, but I can see how his trust in me is directly related to how well I'm listening and empathizing.

"I've been observing Andy in his play therapy sessions."

"That's great practice."

"But he had his last session this week."

"So, he's all done with therapy?"

"His twitching has stopped completely, and it seemed like our sword fight was the last session that really brought out his subconscious emotions. Since then we have just been playing, and Samantha doesn't seem to think his playing is about anything in particular. It's like he doesn't know what else to do. Samantha agreed and said we could stop coming regularly and just check in if we felt we needed to come back."

"Does it feel good to get to this point with Andy? Does he still seem depressed?"

"He doesn't seem depressed anymore. He's not always happy, but it seems like he isn't carrying the weight of the world on his shoulders."

"That's great."

"Yeah, it is."

My voice trails off and I slouch a little. My tone of voice is not matching my uplifting news. I know she recognizes it the moment it comes out.

"So, what's wrong?"

I think back to my twelve step meeting. I hadn't wanted to go this week, and I was trying to get out of it, but I forced myself there.

"I went to my twelve step meeting this week."

She looks at me and waits.

"I thought I was going to go through these twelve steps in couple of months and be done."

A small smile curls up on one side of her mouth, but she represses it.

"I didn't want to go to my meeting, but I went anyway. There was a new person there. She talked about having eight years of sobriety when she stopped going to meetings because she thought she was cured. But as soon as she stopped going to meetings she started drinking again, and rather than starting up where she left off, she said she started drinking at a point way further than where she had left off. She said her drinking had progressed as if she had never quit."

Jen sits still. She turns her head slightly to the side and looks at me.

I take a deep breath.

"It scared me."

"You are a very goal-oriented person, so it will probably be hard for you to accept that this is a lifelong disease. Going to meetings will help you stop drinking, and doing your therapy will help you cope with life without drinking, but none of this will cure alcoholism."

"We heard that in one of our videos, but there was so much information that it didn't sink in."

I think about all the videos and sessions we sat through for inpatient and outpatient treatment. They were all very fascinating and helped me understand what was going on in my head, but I must have decided not to hear the part that said my struggle with this would never end. My heart is sinking. I can't do this for the rest of my life. I hear a verse go through my head. "Be still and know that I am God." (Psalm 46:10) I hate that verse. I feel like the only thing I ever hear from God now is to be still! I hate being still!

"Like every disease, there is some grief in accepting it. Your alcoholism is a little like cancer. You can't just do a few things and be cured. You can only do what is in your power and then leave the rest to God."

I'm quiet. Acceptance again. It's always about accepting things as they are. It's so depressing. I think about my conversation with Nancy after Bible study. She is no longer the director of our Women's Ministry at church. She'd been in that position since I first joined that church, and in my mind she is synonymous with Women's Ministry. It's weird to think she won't be leading it anymore. It's more than weird. It causes me a lot of anxiety, because it's a big change for me. I thought I liked change, but the only change I seem to like is when I'm making the changes. I think about the skills I'm learning and instead of letting my anxiety control my thoughts and actions, I'm forcing myself to think effective thoughts;

something that will help me understand the change and accept it.

"You might see things negatively because you're uncomfortable with change, but you are creating a brand new life; a better one for you and your kids. Things won't be the same as they were, but that is a good thing."

"I know logically it's a good thing, but there are parts of my old life I want back, and I don't think it's going to happen."

"How are things with JB?"

I think about our last communication success in the kitchen.

"It is going better. He is really trying to help me understand what he is saying. Like yesterday he opened the mail and said we don't have any money. He immediately looked at me and said he was not saying that I had spent it all. He was just making a comment. I appreciated him clarifying because what I heard him say was, 'You spent all our money.' I realized that was my own interpretation, not the truth. So, I had to tell myself that he was just making a comment. It was kind of cool, because I could actually feel resentment leaving my body as I listened to him and told myself that was the truth."

"That is an incredible start to good communication! If you guys can keep doing that, you are on your way to really understanding each other, and you won't have to ever let that resentment build again now that you know where it comes from."

"Yeah, it was really good. I could tell we both felt like we got somewhere with it."

I think about the rest of my week because it seemed there were a couple of milestones.

"I also made dinner this week and was able to do it without beating myself up."

"Awesome! How did you do that?"

"We were in a hurry and I was making a frozen pizza. At first I thought about what a terrible mom I am for making pizza again! But I caught myself and told myself to be more positive. I told myself that it's okay to make frozen pizza. We were in a hurry and didn't have time to make anything else and it was no big deal."

"That is tremendous progress, Jenny!"

"Thanks."

I smile. It is huge progress. I can't believe I said something positive about myself. It's a weird feeling. I thought being nice to myself would make me a worse person because I was letting myself get away with something, but it actually makes me feel better because I accepted myself for who I am right now. This feeling of satisfaction is foreign. It makes me restless, like there's nowhere to go because I'm already there. I wonder if this is what peace feels like.

Session 21

I'm in the bathroom of Jen's office building. I'm staring at myself in the mirror. I've never been able to look at myself for long. I force myself to keep looking at the face staring back at me. It's like having a staring contest with a stranger. I tell myself that I need to get to know this person because I'm stuck with her. I don't really want to get to know her, but I think I'm willing to try.

I check my watch and head down the hallway. I'm holding a bag with my calendar, my notes, and a pen. It's been three weeks since I've seen Jen. With the holidays and then Jen going out of town, she thought it was a good idea to let me go a little longer. I was scared, but I had her e-mail and phone number, so I decided I could make it. I don't want to be the creepy client who calls her at home, but my fear of being abandoned is stronger than my desire to not be creepy. I go in the door and the bell rings.

"Come in, Jenny!"

I think it's cool we have the same name. It's such a common name that I don't even notice a lot of the time, but with Jen, I'm happy to have something in common. I go in and sit on the couch. She puts some paperwork away in her drawer and sits in her little brown arm chair. She smiles at me with her usual expectancy. The energy she has today is emanating from her body and I can't help but feel it. She scoots around in her chair as if getting ready to hear a really great adventure story. I guess in a way, that's what I'm giving her.

"So, how was your Christmas?"

"The holidays are always a little crazy. The kids had school off, of course, which was nice, but it made it hard to find any quiet time. So, it was a little stressful."

"Did you use some of your DBT skills to deal with the stress?"

"Yes, I did. I decided to keep things simple. Like I put up fewer decorations and tried to spend more time playing with my kids. I went to my twelve step group which always makes me feel better."

"And how did you do with your extended families?"

"We always spend Christmas Eve with my in-laws. I don't worry about alcohol with them because they are very supportive, and they don't drink unless they are entertaining, so I didn't have to worry about that side. On Christmas day my family came over. I've been providing wine with dinner in years past, so I told them this year we weren't going to have any alcohol in the house."

"How did they do with that?"

"It's hard to tell, because no one in my family likes confrontation, so no one actually argues, except for my dad. He likes to start arguments; usually about religion, but I handled him better this year than usual."

Jen sits up in her chair as she listens.

I'm sitting on the couch watching TV while everyone is playing games and talking and eating. My dad is on a chair across from me. I try not to look at him, but he is staring at me. It feels a little like he has spotted his prey from his deer stand. He begins his hunt.

"Jenny!"

He says it loudly over the TV and all the other conversations going on. I look at him because I know if I ignore him he will just say it louder next time.

"What are your kids learning at church about Christmas?"

I look at him out of the corner of my eye, like a deer in the forest that is alert to some unknown danger.

"What do you mean?"

My dad's gun is loaded, and he's stalking me in order to aim his gun before I run.

"Like what are you teaching your kids?"

I fall for the bait and reply. I try to keep it simple so I don't leave too much of myself exposed.

"We're teaching them about Jesus."

He holds the gun steady as he looks through the site.

"Well, how do you know that's true what you're teaching them? Ain't it different than what your mom and brother believe? How do you know what's right?"

The tone of his voice is mocking. He has my heart between the cross hairs on his site. I sit still for a moment listening and thinking. Normally I try to come up with the best logical answer I can give him, but I realize that he doesn't want an answer from me. He only wants to get my attention long enough that I will sit still for him so he can get his shot off. I don't know why it took me so long to figure this out, but now that I have, I decide I'm not going to sit still so he can frustrate and hurt me. I begin an elusive maneuver.

"I'm teaching my kids about having a relationship with God."

He begins laying out some bait; a little pile of corn to entice me toward him.

"What do you mean a relationship? Like he's their friend! How can someone be a friend if you can't see them?"

I avoid the bait and stay under the cover of the forest trees.

"I don't know all the answers, and I can't remember all the facts that I've read, but I know God is real because he talks to me."

I think back to my last year and all the times I knew God was talking to me directly, leaving no doubt in my mind.

239

My Dad's arm slips a little and he tries to get the cross hairs lined up again. I think he was expecting a different answer, some statement of factual nature that he could logically blow out of the sky. He re-aims and cocks the gun.

"Well, God ain't never talked to me!"

I can tell he thinks his shot was aimed well. Even though he had to realign, he is expecting to hit his target, because he's never missed in the past. He's probably even feeling a big adrenaline rush knowing he has caught up to me, that I wasn't able to move away from his line of sight. What he doesn't know is that I don't have to play his games anymore. I don't feel the need to solve all of his problems or anyone's for that matter. God is big enough to deal with my dad. So, I answer him with as much pity as I can muster.

"Wow Dad, that's too bad."

I turn to watch the television again. I'm not really watching the program. I'm just ignoring him. He's silent. He can't believe his perfect aim didn't strike the target. I can tell he doesn't know what to do now that I'm not willing to play into his game. I feel better than I've felt in a long time.

I relay this story to Jen.

"Wow! Have you ever done that before with your dad?"

"No. I always fall into his trap and then get mad and frustrated as I watch him get more and more excited. This time I just let it all go. I thought about me and what I need to do for me, and it worked!"

"Do you see how what you did was draw a boundary line for yourself?"

Actually I didn't know what I did. I just knew it felt good. I look at Jen to explain more.

"Refusing to play his game was drawing a boundary line for yourself, and as long as you don't let him drag you over that boundary line, you can protect yourself."

I wrinkle my eyebrows and stare at her chair processing her words.

"You can't control what your dad says or does, but you can control how you feel by controlling what you say and do. You can do this with anyone about anything."

I feel exhilarated. I still feel the excitement of eluding my dad's shot and the freedom of knowing I can draw a boundary line with anyone. I understand that I don't have to be drawn into something if I don't want to. I don't have to be controlled by other people's actions and feelings and words. I can control my part in something and I don't have to get involved at all if I don't want to. It seems so backwards. Letting go of control has actually given me more control. I look at Jen with a big smile on my face. She smiles back as we share another winning moment on the battle field of my mind.

Session 22

It's been four weeks. Jen wants me to start stretching myself and going longer between sessions. I know it's good for me, but I don't like it. I walk down the hall and into her office. I sit on the couch and smile. It feels good to sink into the familiar brown cushions.

"How are you?"

"I'm doing ok."

"Great. How did your last few weeks go?"

My mind is blank. Four weeks is so long.

"It feels like I haven't been here in a long time."

"I bet it does."

Jen is quiet. It's the sign that she wants to know more. I breathe.

"I know I can't be here forever, but when I'm at home and things seem overwhelming, I feel better knowing I only have so many more days before my appointment. I'm kind of afraid of how I will do when I don't have an appointment to look forward to anymore."

"You know you can come in anytime. It's good to check in once in a while."

My hands and arms drop to my side and my stomach stops turning. I let out a deep breath.

"So, what have you been up to?"

My mind is clearer as I attempt to remember my last four weeks.

"You know I've been going to a Bible study."

"Yes, I remember."

"Some things came together for me last week."

"What was that?"

"My mom raised us in the Mormon Church where there were a lot of rules to follow and a lot of pressure to follow them. If you didn't live up to the church's expectations you were looked down upon because you weren't going to make it to the highest level of heaven. In my Bible study we drew out a timeline and wrote down all the religious-oriented events that have happened in our lives. Then we wrote down any memorable life events, good or bad that happened to us along the same timeline. That was when I realized that my rape happened about the same age that my expectations in my church were raised. I was introduced to the goals of a teenager in the Mormon Church, and I knew my future depended on my ability to follow all the rules. Being raped made me feel like I blew any chance of ever accomplishing those goals. With my competitive spirit and need for recognition, I don't think anything could have stopped me from becoming the best, most committed Mormon I could possibly be. If I had continued to grow up as a totally committed Mormon I can't see how I would have ever understood the meaning of grace. And without grace, I wouldn't have been able to build the relationship I have with Jesus. Even though I've been mad at God, the relationship I have with him is worth more to me than being raped."

I take a deep breath.

"I don't know for sure that this is why God let it happen, but the idea that maybe there are reasons too big for me to understand makes me feel better about it."

My struggle with God over being raped reminds me of Andy's struggle with me during his therapy. I feel like I had my own sword fight with God. I imagine that God, being the creator of the universe, doesn't owe me an explanation of why things happen, yet he handed me a sword like I handed Andy a sword. And just like I let Andy stab me over and over so he knew I understood his pain, God let me stab him over and over until I knew that he understood my pain. But where I *pretended* to feel the pain from Andy's sword, God let me hurt him for real when he let his son die on a cross. I've always wondered why God would make a plan of salvation by letting his son be tortured and killed. Maybe it was so we know that God cares enough to understand our pain in the most real way we can imagine. What could be worse than watching your child be tortured and killed? I feel like another cloak has been lifted off my shoulders only this one was made of chainmail.

"So, how do you feel?"

"Less angry, more peaceful."

"That's really great insight."

We both smile enjoying another positive step forward in my progress.

"And how are things going with JB?"

"It's not perfect, but our communication is miles from where it started. He is more aware of how I interpret what he says, so he's been careful about explaining what he means when he makes a random comment. And I have learned to stop and think logically about what he says before I jump to conclusions. It's still not easy to do, but when something he says triggers me emotionally, I repeat his words to myself and logically walk through them."

I walk into the kitchen. JB is sitting at the table reading the paper. He asks where I was. I grit my jaw and crease my eyebrows as I begin to think of a hundred ways to tell him to mind his own business because I can go anywhere I want without having to tell him every single detail. I'm suddenly aware of my anger. It's a red flag, so I stop myself to think about why I'm angry. I'm beginning to recognize that my anger is not always what it appears to be. I read too much into what JB is saying. I let this roll around in my mind for a moment and wonder if he's just simply asking me where I was rather than demanding to know where I was and why I thought I could do something without his permission.

I decide to push my anger aside for a minute and pretend that he isn't reprimanding me. He is just curious. I tell him I was at the bookstore. He doesn't look up from the paper. He starts talking about one of the articles he's reading. I'm not really hearing anything he is saying because I'm thinking about how chaotic I almost made a simple conversation. I can't believe I've been doing that for so many years! I'm relieved we're not arguing, and the tension in my shoulders evaporates as I listen to an ordinary conversation. I wonder if normal couples have chats like this every day about the news and work and kids and family. It's so nice.

"That is amazing. It might be hard, but I think the longer you practice that exercise, the easier it will become."

It's hard to think about communication becoming easier. I know everything gets easier with practice, but calling communication easy is a big stretch for me.

"How are your kids doing?"

My mind drifts to last night.

I'm walking into the house with my arms full of groceries. Johnny meets me at the door with his usual high energy.

"Mom! Will you play football with me?"

I look at the groceries and think about dinner and the laundry. Everything in me wants to clean and organize and catch up with my never ending "to do" list. I remember my promise to myself to put everything down when my kids ask me to do something, and I tell myself everything else can wait.

"Yes, we can. I just have to put away the cold things."

I follow Johnny outside and we line up in the back yard. I'm the quarterback. Johnny is the wide receiver. He has already taught me what to say and how to hike the ball. We've been working on plays this week. My job is to throw the ball just out of his reach so he can make some diving catches. This is not an easy job, but I'm getting better and he hasn't fired me yet. We run play after play until it gets dark. He wants one more good one. I drop back and throw it just as he turns to cut across the field. He leaps and catches it in his fingertips falling into the end zone. He does one of his touchdown dances, and we high five on our way in.

We walk into the house to find Andy at the kitchen table writing something. He is working on a poem for English. He likes to write, so he's always working on English homework. He sees me and tells me to wait because he's almost finished, and he wants me to read it. I'm anxious to get to my chores, but I know a writer's heart is fragile, so I sit at the table next to him. I look at his expression. His eyebrows wrinkle together. He nods his head as he searches for the right word. He finishes it and smiles as he slides it toward me. I read the poem.

> *Sometimes you're happy.*
> *Sometimes you're sad.*
> *Sometimes you're just really mad.*
> *Sometimes it's just a thought.*
> *That is very hardly fought.*
> *Sometimes it takes determination.*
> *Sometimes it's just in your imagination.*

He writes about life like he's been through a lot already. Compared to other kids his age, I guess he has. I feel a

247

twinge of guilt. I always do when I see an emotional scar left from my drinking. He wants to write movies. I want him to get better grades in math in case his writing career doesn't take off, but I don't want to deflate his dream. He'll have plenty of critics. He needs me to encourage him. I'm determined to be his biggest fan.

It's getting late, so I tell everyone to get ready for bed. After tucking in Andy and Johnny, I go to Jenna's room. I kneel by her bed and we say our prayers. She scooches over to make room and pats the bed next to her. That's my sign. I crawl in. I ask her about school and friends. She tells me what she did at school as I put my arm underneath her head. She is talking and I'm not only listening, but I notice that I'm listening. I notice that after years of self-absorbed parenting and months of therapy, I am lying down by my daughter and she is telling me about her day, and I am listening. I'm not thinking about tomorrow or yesterday or all the things on my "to do" list. I'm thinking about the classes she is talking about, and I'm picturing which of her friends she mentions. Being aware that I am making a conscious choice to be an active participant in her life makes me think of myself at her age. It's a bittersweet thought. On one hand my heart aches wishing I had someone that would listen to me and know everything about me. On the other hand I am overwhelmingly grateful to have a chance to really know my daughter.

My eyes are so heavy all I want to do is crawl into my own bed and fall asleep, but I relish every word she says, because I know how many I've missed in the past, and I can't imagine how many words I might have missed in the future if I hadn't learned how to pay attention. Thinking about how much I wish I had been held at her age, I wrap her up tight in my arms and smile as we drift off to sleep.

Time I spend with my kids now is like little treasures. Every time I give them my complete attention I build a little bridge over the brick wall that had kept us so far apart. I didn't realize they had been trying to build that bridge all along. I feel incredibly blessed that they never stopped trying.

"I've been making it a habit to sit down and listen to my kids, and it's been really cool. I don't feel like they're so far away anymore."

"They are very lucky to have you as their mom."

I'm not sure lucky is the word I would have used.

"I think you've come a long way from where you started. And you have the tools you need to deal with life situations. What do you think about spreading out your sessions to every other month? It doesn't mean you are done or that you can't come back sooner. It just means I think you're ready to try out your skills on your own. How do you feel about that?"

I didn't want her to say that, but I knew it was coming. It feels like learning to ride my bike. We've taken off the training wheels, and she's been running alongside me while I wobble down the road. I'm getting the hang of it though and wobbling less, and now it's time for her to stop running alongside me.

"I'm willing to try it."

"Great, but remember you can call me if you want to come in sooner, or you feel your medication isn't working or anything that you're concerned about."

"Okay."

I grab my purse and notebook. Knowing I can come back makes me feel safe and a little braver. I walk down the long hallway and rather than heading to the parking lot I push open the door to the women's bathroom. I set my things on the counter and look into the mirror. I notice bits of grey hair trying to blend in with the sandy blond ones, and the smile lines around my mouth, and wrinkles forming around my eyes. I have heard that eyes are the windows to our soul. As I look into my eyes I see the frightened mom who walked into a treatment center, and the teenager who wondered if anyone really cared, and the young girl who sharpened her knife blade and carved a wooden heart to replace the soft one she lost. I'm used to seeing these images of myself, but in between the grey hair and wrinkles, there's a new person looking back at me. She tells me that I'm going to have to begin to see the positive in myself instead of just the negative, because my kids are following in my footsteps, especially my daughter, Jenna.

If there's anything I've learned over the last year it's that we copy what we see and hear from our parents. Jenna will become her own person, but there is no way around her picking up many aspects of who I am. So, I know that I need to learn to love myself in order for her to learn how to love herself. And I need to stand up for myself if I want her to learn to stand up for herself. And I need to be a happy, successful woman with a purpose in my life if I ever hope for her to be a happy, successful woman with a purpose. I know her future isn't entirely up to me, but I also know my choices will influence her, and I can definitely leave fewer hurdles for her to jump than my mom left for me.

As I look at this new image of myself in the mirror, I'm not sure if I can love her immediately, but I can start by being nice to her. And as I let go of my judgments about her, her years of struggle look less like baggage and more like wisdom. And the recovering alcoholic label she carries looks less like shame and more like strength. And the disorganized mess of a housewife looks less like failure and more like the unique, artistic woman that her family is lucky to have.

I smile at the thought of my family being lucky to have me. For some reason I'm embarrassed by that kind of self-assurance. At the same time I know that in many ways it's true. I imagine my kids with all their gifts and talents, starting out their lives in a much different place than I did. I imagine that instead of a long, lonely road full of trap doors and quick sand, they'll have a paved highway with road signs and rest stops. Instead of walking with a limp, they'll be driving a fast car or maybe riding a horse or flying a plane. I'm not naïve enough to think they won't have problems, because no one gets through life without them. But I'm proud of the work I've done to give them a better starting point than they might have had otherwise, and if I have to learn to love myself in the process, that's not such a bad thing.

It reminds me of a Bible verse that Nancy has drilled into my head over the last year. "We know that in all things God works for the good of those who love him, who have been called according to his purpose." (Romans 8:28)

251

When I hear that verse I wonder if I've been called to something because I don't feel like I have a purpose, but when Jen and Nancy and Ann and JB all point out how far I've come and how much work I've done in the past year, I realize I don't have to be in some high position in the business world or my church to have a calling and a purpose. If my only purpose is to stop the patterns of addiction in my family so my kids don't have to carry that burden into their adult lives, then I am probably making just as much a contribution to our world as any big business or church leader, and that's enough. But I think there's more.

What if I could share my story with people and they realized they had a choice about whether or not they are going to pass on the bad habits of their parents or begin a new family tradition? And what if hundreds or even thousands of kids' lives were better because their parents were courageous enough to change? It's almost too much to hope for, but just like one rock can make ripples that spread out across the water, I'd like to believe that maybe one decision could change the world.

Made in the USA
Charleston, SC
29 November 2012